The
Sports
Parenting
Edge

The

Sports
Parenting
Edge

by
Rick Wolff

RUNNING PRESS
PHILADELPHIA · LONDON

9   8   7   6   5   4   3   2   1
Digit on the right indicates the number of this printing

Library of Congress Control Number 2002117806

ISBN 0-7624-1589-4

Cover designed by Whitney Cookman
Cover photograph by © Jim Whitmer/ Getty Images
Interior designed by Serrin Bodmer
Edited by Greg Jones
Typography: Bodoni and GillSans

This book may be ordered by mail from the publisher.
Please include $2.50 for postage and handling.
But try your bookstore first!

Running Press Book Publishers
125 South Twenty-second Street
Philadelphia, Pennsylvania 19103-4399

Visit us on the web!
www.runningpress.com

CONTENTS

ACKNOWLEDGMENTS

This book was the original brainchild of my long-time friend and trusted publishing colleague, Carlo DeVito. As a new parent himself and life-long sports fan, Carlo instinctively knew that the road to happiness in sports these days is a lot more complicated than it was when we were growing up. So, Carlo, my friend, my thanks to you for providing the inspiration.

Once the idea was born, my editor Greg Jones was absolutely instrumental in bringing this book to life. I know firsthand how difficult it can be to keep an author on track in terms of publishing deadlines, and Greg did an absolutely splendid job in making sure I got all the words down on paper on time. Thank you, Greg, as well as all the other fine folks at Running Press.

Of course, my own involvement in sports parenting came from watching my own three children become involved in sports. Whether it was baseball, swimming, soccer, ice hockey, or lacrosse, I want to personally thank my kids—John, Alyssa, and Samantha—for allowing me to watch them grow and develop in their respective sports. And of course, the real expert in sports parenting is my wonderful wife, Trish. She's the one who teaches me about kids—especially when I'm acting like a kid myself. Thank you, Trish!

I also want to thank my own Mom and Dad. Way back when I was a kid playing ball on the sandlots, little did I know that they were gently teaching me all the basics of sports parenting. Their worthy insights and good solid advice have served me for years, and have always been the foundation of all my work in this field. Thanks Mom and Dad!

Finally, I want to take a moment to thank all of the other Moms and Dads who serve as giving and dedicated sports parents, and who have been kind enough to either call me on my weekly radio show on WFAN, or to email me at the Center for Sports Parenting, or to write to me via my columns through *Sports Illustrated*. Your input and observations teach me more and more about sports parenting every day, and I thank you for your warm advice and counsel.

Sports is still supposed to be about having fun. To me, that's always been the first as well as the last word when it comes to sports. I sincerely hope we can keep it that way for our kids, and for our kids' kids.

Rick Wolff
April 2003

INTRODUCTION

The First Question Every Sports Parent Has to Ask. . . .

Very simply, that question is:

What do you really want your child to get out of sports?

It's a fairly straightforward question, but if you're like most parents who want their kid involved in sports, it's not always that easy a question to answer. For example, if your goal is for your child to someday become a professional or Olympic-caliber athlete, you had better come to realize early on in the parenting process that the odds of any of that happening are microscopically small. In the 21st century, there are literally millions of kids in this country (not to mention the world) who share those dreams—and of course, their parents share those dreams as well.

"Okay," you say, "maybe being an Olympic or pro athlete is a bit too much to wish for. But it sure would be nice if my kid was good enough to get an athletic scholarship to college. . . ." Well, that's a fine dream, too. But you should know that the odds of that happening are also drastically stacked against your son or daughter. There are precious few athletic scholarships to be offered, and once again, there are millions of kids seeking them.

Let me present these odds in another way. When I coached college baseball at Mercy College in Dobbs Ferry, NY (an NCAA Division II school), I had a small number of athletic scholarships to hand out each year. To fill these scholarships, I could literally pick and choose ballplayers from all over the tri-state New York/New Jersey/Connecticut area.

Mercy College is located in Westchester County, where there are approximately 55 high schools plus a number of private and parochial schools. Right across the Hudson River is Rockland County, NY, where there are another 10 high schools. To the east is Fairfield County, CT, where there are approximately 15 to 20 more high schools. Then to the south, there are Nassau and Suffolk Counties, where there are dozens more high schools. And don't forget New Jersey, where there are even more schools to choose from. In effect, I could choose to recruit ballplayers from 200+ high schools in this 50-mile radius. And I could recruit top players from local junior colleges as well.

Now, in every one of these high schools, there are star baseball players who are named Captain, or All-League, or All-County, or All-something. They are all fine high school baseball players. But I would only have to choose two or three a year to fit my needs at Mercy. So, the odds went something like this: if I needed to find a good shortstop, I could look at more than 200 high school shortstops each year to find just one and offer him a scholarship.

That's one out of 200+ outstanding high school or junior college shortstops. And that was for little ol' Mercy College.

I think—I hope—I've made my point. If you really want to get your kid a scholarship for college, you're better off hoping that they get one for academics, not for sports.

So again, the question is posed:

What do you really want your child to get out of sports?

How about setting some more basic—and more reachable—goals? Like hoping that your child simply develops a lifelong love for athletic exercise that will keep them physically fit for the rest of their life? And that they learn the lessons of hard work, discipline, and sacrifice that are the foundation for living life beyond their sports years? And that they enjoy the overall experience of working hard with teammates and competing against their opponents? And finally, that they become proficient enough in their sports that they might enjoy that magical moment of scoring the winning goal, or of being on a championship team, or of just knowing that they've worked hard at their skills and have become a very, very good athlete?

This book is designed to help children who play sports—and their parents who encourage them and cheer them on—to pursue all of those goals. Yes, a few special ones may go on to become professional or college competitors, but statistics tell us that only a very small percentage of high school varsity athletes ever go on to play college sports. And an even smaller percentage of college athletes are good enough to be tapped to play in the professional ranks. And even at the professional ranks, the average playing career of all athletes is rarely more than a few years. In other words, the entire athletic experience lasts a relatively short period of time.

Essential Parenting Tip: Pack Two Parachutes

As a sports parent, it's up to you to act like an adult, and be the grown-up that you now are. **Suggestion:** take a tip from paratroopers who jump out of airplanes for a living. They always pack a backup parachute in case the first one doesn't open. You should give the same advice to your child as well. Tell your son or daughter to pack two parachutes in life. The first parachute is their dream to become a star athlete. The second backup parachute is to be used in case that first dream doesn't come true. And as their parent, it's up to you to be totally supportive of all their dreams.

Ideally, that secondary or backup dream will reflect another passion they have in life as well, whether it be a desire to become a teacher, fire fighter, coach, doctor, whatever. But that second parachute should always be tucked away in the back of their mind as they progress through their school athletic years.

A BREAKDOWN OF THE
ODDS OF "MAKING IT"

What are the current stats on aspiring high school kids who want to advance in sports? Here are some recent numbers as compiled by the NCAA and other sources:

Football: Only 9 out of every 10,000 high school senior football players will eventually be drafted by an NFL team. Less than 4% of all high school football players ever play college football, and less than 1% of college players ever make it to the NFL.

Boys Basketball: About 3 out of every 10,000 high school senior basketball players will eventually be drafted by an NBA team.

Odds: 3,333 to 1.

Or, look at it this way: For every 2,300 high school senior basketball players, only 40 will play college basketball, and only one of those will get a chance at the NBA.

Girls Basketball: Only one out of 5,000 senior girls playing high school basketball will be drafted by the WNBA.

Odds: 5,000 to 1.

Baseball: Maybe one out of 200 high school seniors will be selected in the Major League draft.

Odds: 200 to 1.

Ice Hockey: One out of every 250 high school seniors will be tapped by a team in the National Hockey League draft.

Odds: 250 to 1.

Gymnastics: More than two million kids participate in gymnastics each year, but only seven or eight participate in the Olympic games every four years.

Want even more sobering information? The vast majority of kids who are lucky enough to be drafted professionally will never get close to actually playing in the NBA, WNBA, NFL, Major Leagues, or the NHL. There are just too many other players for too few slots, not to mention the possibility of injuries and other unforeseen setbacks.

When I worked with the Cleveland Indians as their roving sports performance enhancement coach, I used to do the math in my head. At the start of each year, we would have 120 or so pro ballplayers report to spring training in February. But come June, we would also draft and sign another 30 or more new players. How did we make all the players fit? We didn't. Quite simply, each year, the Indians—like every other professional organization—would have to release (or fire) 30 current ballplayers to make room for the new ones. And of course, this process was repeated each year. In short, it was built into the system that 30 players would see their careers come to an end each spring.

Now, of those 120 players in the minor league system, what were the odds of any of them ever getting "a cup of coffee" (a short stay) in the big leagues? No more than 10–15%. In other words, just because you were good enough to get drafted and signed was no guarantee that you'd play in the majors. The odds were still 90% against you of getting to the big leagues, even if you were already a pro.

In short, Mom and Dad, do all that you can for your kids in sports, but make certain your son and daughter pack two parachutes.

I wrote this book to help educate Moms and Dads to understand just how difficult it is to have one's son or daughter climb the slippery slope of the athletic pyramid of competition. But even more importantly, I also wrote it so that young athletes everywhere can make the most out of their God-given abilities and have the most fun they can have out of playing sports.

THE SEVEN BIGGEST
MYTHS AND MISCONCEPTIONS
ABOUT YOUTH SPORTS

1. Some travel teams start for kids as young as age 6 or 7. The sooner you can get your child to play on this kind of team, the better.
2. All travel team coaches are certified educators, have degrees in physical education or psychology, and have a solid background in coaching kids.
3. Once your child chooses one sport to specialize in, that will give him or her a better chance of advancing to a higher level (e.g., college, professional ranks).
4. The best time to teach your youngster how to improve their play is immediately after the game—ideally, in the car ride on the way home when their actions are still fresh in their mind.
5. A youngster who is a top athlete among his or her peers at age 8 is clearly destined to be a star when they're 18.
6. Creatine as well as other nutritional supplements that are sold in health stores have all been proven to be safe for your child; otherwise, it would be illegal for the stores to sell them.
7. The vast majority of Moms and Dads tend to be honest and fairly objective about their child's ability in sports.

MATCH QUIZ

Match the Athlete with Their Sports Background

A. Michael Jordan	1. Played only basketball in college at Arizona
B. Larry Walker	2. Was only 5'11" as a senior in high school
C. Kenny Lofton	3. Got cut from his high school hoops team
D. Cynthia Cooper	4. Wanted to be a pro hockey goalie but got cut
E. Scottie Pippen	5. Didn't start playing ball until 14
F. Sammy Sosa	6. Didn't start playing ball until 16
G. Mark McGwire	7. Outstanding goalkeeper in soccer
H. Hakeem Olajuwon	8. Was a top college basketball player at UCLA
I. Dan Bylsma	9. Not recruited out of high school
J. John Stockton	10. Never played on a travel team as a kid
K. Jackie Joyner-Kersee	11. Eyesight as a child was 20/500

Answers: A-3; B-4; C-1; D-6; E-2; F-5; G-11; H-7; I-10; J-9; K-8

CHAPTER ONE:
The Early Years

What's the Right Age to Start
My Kid in Sports?

The younger, the better, right?

The truth? No one knows for certain.

If a reputable scientific researcher or a university professor published a paper that proved beyond a shadow of a doubt that starting a youngster in sports at a very early age really, really "worked," then we would all have our children playing soccer by age 2, or hitting a baseball by age 3, or working on their tennis serve by age 4. For that matter, some sports parents would probably have their kid prepping in utero!

But as of this book's publication, to my knowledge there is no such definitive study or paper that suggests starting kids early in sports gives them an edge. Still, there are thousands of parents who feel otherwise; that is, if they can get their kid playing and practicing a sport at an extremely young age, then somehow all that early training will serve as a springboard to greater athletic success in the future.

However, parental experience also dictates that you can't force a youngster to play and enjoy a sport. More importantly, the smart parents know that kids will find the sports that they want to play—not the other way around. These are fundamental observations about starting your child in athletics, but unfortunately, lots of parents either decide to overlook these realities or simply don't want to assume that they're true.

Now all this being said, every so often you'll see a feature story on the television news about a 4-year-old who just hit a hole-in-one at the local country club, or a 5-year-old who just bowled a perfect game, or some other extraordinary athletic accomplishment by a little tyke. The reason why these events are so amazing and newsworthy is because of the age of the youngster. As you might imagine, all of these athletic feats were most likely strongly encouraged by the child's parents. After all, you don't usually find a 4-year-old who is naturally attracted to golf, or a 5-year-old who just happens to fall in love with bowling.

Furthermore, I often wonder whatever happens to these kids as they get older. How many of them actually continue to thrive in athletics as they develop into their teenage years?

Of course, I'm certain that the first thought that comes to your mind is the extraordinary success of Tiger Woods. And yes, it's true that Earl Woods, Tiger's father, had Tiger out on the golf course at a very early age. But that's where most people stop reading the rest of Tiger's story. As Earl has stated many times, he was always very cautious not to push his son to play golf; indeed, some Tiger fans are often surprised to discover that Tiger played other sports as a youngster as well. And Earl was smart enough to know that if he asked Tiger if he wanted to play a round of golf today—and Tiger said no—then Earl never pushed or prodded his son to do so. Earl Woods knew that once a kid is coerced to play a sport, it's at that point where the youngster's fascination with the sport transforms into a chore. **When a sport becomes a chore, that's when the child's inner drive usually diminishes.** That's an important lesson.

The other important lesson here is this: How many Tiger Woods are there in the world of sports? How many other top athletes have you heard about who were child prodigies in their sport and remained a star in that sport right through high school, college, and into the pros? Okay, maybe tennis's Williams sisters—Venus and Serena—but after that, who else? What other top athletes of today can you point to as being well-known examples of kids who started their sport at an extremely young age?

To me, the real challenge in getting a youngster off to the right start in sports is not to inundate with practice, practice, and more practice, but rather to introduce them to a variety of sports in the hope that they might find two or three that they really seem to enjoy. Developing a child's passion for a sport or sports is the key; it's that inner passion that will ultimately serve as a mainspring to keep them driving ahead in their competitive sports.

Remember this: it's not very important that your child is the best soccer player in town at age 5, or the best T-ball player at age 6. To me, the ultimate goal is to first build your child's love for the sport, and if that bond occurs, then perhaps they'll push themselves to be one of the best soccer players or baseball players in school when they're 17 or 18. Indeed, I've written this book based on the premise that the ultimate goal is to develop young athletes to make the most out of their ability by the time they finish their years in high school.

There's a downside, of course, to pushing a child into sports too young. Athletic burnout does begin to occur in kids any time after the age of 9 or 10. As a concerned sports parent, burnout is something that you want to avoid for your child at all costs. But ironically, the seeds of burnout are usually planted in the child when they start sports at a very early age.

Why does athletic burnout occur in kids? No one has a precise answer to this question, although my suspicion is that these kids start to peak at an early age, then become a little bored with their sport, and then go on to find other activities in life. Here's a statistic that I often refer to in my talks with sports parents, and it's something that every parent has to bear in mind: According to the Michigan State Institute for Youth Sports, **of all the kids who play organized sports in this country, by the time they reach the age of 13, 74% of them will quit.**

That's a frightening number. That means that 3 out of 4 kids will stop playing organized sports by the time they're entering junior high school. Now, it's to be expected that some children, as they get older, will normally find that their interests in life go beyond the athletic fields. After all, as kids begin to explore their world, they may find that they love performing on the stage rather than being on the soccer team, or they find that they would rather be involved in school government than play softball. This is all fine and certainly understandable. But no one would expect the percentage of young athletes who quit sports to be as high as 74 percent!

How Do You Build Passion? Try a Little Praise

Before you sign your kid up for the local peewee soccer team or basketball squad, your first job as a sports parent is to let a sense of passion develop within your child. Never take this step for granted, because if the sport ever transforms for your youngster from being "enjoyable fun" into a "mandatory obligation," I can assure you that your child will be one of those kids who end up walking away from their sport in their early teenage years.

So how does one encourage and allow a passion for a sport to grow within a youngster? For the most part, it's very simple. Just let your child find the sport (or sports) that they are naturally attracted to, and let them go out and embrace it **in their own way**. That's a key phrase, because when a 4- or 5-year-old first starts to dribble a basketball or tries to throw a football or attempts to kick a soccer ball, they're going to want to be able to do it in their own childlike way and fashion. Kids that young don't want to be encumbered or restricted by a parent who's only too eager to provide detailed instruction on the proper way to swing a bat or throw a ball. And kids that young are not going to respond terribly well to parents who want them to practice their sports skills over and over again.

It's like letting a kid learn to play a piano. If you inform your 5-year-old that, starting tomorrow, they're going to be taking piano lessons from

Mrs. Figglesworth every Tuesday and Thursday after school, it's a sure bet your kid will start his piano playing experience with great reluctance. After all, you just took the fun out of playing the piano—you've now made it into a twice-a-week chore. After only a few practice sessions, your young pianist will be counting the minutes until the lesson is over so that they can go out and just have fun with the other kids.

On the other hand, if you're lucky enough to have a piano in your house and your child shows some interest in it by occasionally plunking the keys with great pleasure, you can start angling your child toward regular practice by praising his or her natural affection for the piano. Then you can ask your youngster if they would like to take a few lessons. If the child's face brightens with excitement, then you know it's time to call Mrs. Figglesworth. Why? Because it's the child who has developed his or her own spark, or passion, for the piano, rather than having it thrust on them.

Sound simple? It is. It's all in the way you approach your child. Try a little praise and watch your kid's eyes light up. Indeed one of the nice by-products of praise is that it promotes passion.

This same approach works for sports. There's no use or sense in trying to push or prod your youngster into playing a sport at a very early age unless they come to you and tell you that they're eager to play ball. That being said, if you happen to see your son or daughter kicking a soccer ball well, there's nothing wrong with giving them a little parental encouragement and praise. But after that, let them develop their own passion for sports—because unless they develop that inner love for the game, there's nothing to propel the child through all the future years of practices and games. It doesn't matter how much *you* love football, or hockey, or tennis—if your child doesn't have their own enjoyment of that sport, there's really little you can do to help foster that passion. **It has to come from within them—and not from you.**

Okay, They Have the Passion.
Now Where Do We Sign Up?

Let's assume that your youngster can't wait to play soccer. Every day, she can't wait until you come home from work, so that she has someone to pass the ball to. And when you're not home, she's already blasting a soccer ball against the backyard wall. In other words, it's clear she wants to play soccer, and that she wants to play on a team.

What's the right age? Again, there's no hard and fast rule on this. Some organized youth soccer leagues start as young as age 5. (Soccer is usually the first organized team sport that most kids play because the rules of the game are simple, soccer fields are usually plentiful, and the cost of equipment is minimal.) Other sports, such as ice hockey, baseball, basketball, and so on, may also offer local recreational teams for 5- and 6-year-olds. But assuming that your child is raring to go, your next call is to the local town recreational department to find out about youth-level programs.

This is always a good start, because in most communities, the town Rec department is run by professionals who have been educated and trained in the field of physical education. Their job is to provide safe, well-organized youth leagues and basic instruction for kids—especially young kids. They often provide brochures for upcoming clinics, camps, and leagues.

But My Five-Year-Old Wants to Play on a Travel Team

Travel teams, as you may have heard, usually are organized, run, and coached by individual parents who feel that they want their child to play against so-called "better" competition. While there is nothing inherently wrong with travel teams, I do want to caution sports parents that there are some concerns that have to be addressed (see Chapter Four for more details).

But for youngsters starting out in sports, I really don't see any advantage at all to be playing on a travel team. First off, how in the world does anyone know which 6-year-old or 7-year-old is a "better" player than another kid that age? At those very tender ages, kids are just learning the very basic fundamentals of position on the field, of how to kick a ball, and quite frankly, of how to be a team member and listen to a coach.

Don't underestimate how important these cognitive issues are for a kid. Learning to be a team member, for example, is a major leap for any youngster. Bear in mind that children grow up in an environment where they see themselves as the absolute center of their world. (Remember how hard it was to teach your kid how to share with others?) This is part of a normal and healthy childhood. But when they join a team of peers for the first time, kids have to learn how to give up control of the ball and pass it to a teammate. That can be quite challenging for a young player—especially a young and talented one. Hence, it makes a lot of sense to allow them to learn these basic parts of team play while they're on their local rec or organized youth-league team.

In addition, travel teams at this age basically require that your child commit to more practices each week, and more games on the weekend. Again, be careful with this, especially if your child wants to play more than one sport. Many kids, especially when just starting out, don't know which sport or sports they want to pursue. So they'll sign up for football, soccer, hockey, basketball, and so on, in the hopes that Mom or Dad can chauffeur them to all the practices.

Fortunately, as kids get a little older, they'll begin to start choosing which sports they want to stay with. But if they're already locked into just one sport—in our example, just soccer—how would they ever know that they might have liked football or basketball even more?

The bottom line? There's no need to worry about travel teams for your youngsters until they're around the age of 9 or 10. Around that time they will have developed a stronger sense of self-esteem, as well as a sense of how they match up with their athletic peers. Plus they will have developed a certain mastery of the skills necessary to excel in their sport.

But If He Doesn't Play Travel, He Won't Catch Up!

Nonsense!

This is one of the numerous myths that surround the development of young athletes. It's the mistaken sense that if your child doesn't opt for a travel team when they're 6 or 8 or even 10, then they're destined to "fall behind the athletic curve" in their peer group and will never be able to catch up with all the other kids who do play on a travel squad.

I call this syndrome "trying to keep up with the athletic Joneses in the neighborhood," and I fully understand that it comes from nervous sports parents who are worried that they may be holding back or even quashing their kid's athletic career if they don't put them on a travel team at a very early age.

Let me reassure you that at ages below 10, whether your child plays—or doesn't play—on a travel team probably won't have much impact on their future athletic development. Why? Because at those very young ages, kids are still just learning their basic skills, rules, positions, and strategies of how to play the game. More importantly, during the elementary school years, they haven't experienced any major growth spurts. These kinds of significant physical changes, such as growing tall, or becoming stronger, or faster, will have a major impact on their athletic development in their teenage years. But those years are still several years off into the future.

In fact, at this age level, one can even make a strong argument that it might be more beneficial for a youngster to play on a rec team rather than a travel team. Why? Because it's good for a child to develop a strong sense of self-confidence by playing—and doing well—against their same-age peers. A child's self-confidence may not have a chance to develop, ironically, if the youngster is playing on a travel team where all the kids are highly talented.

For example, let's say your child happens to be physically average in size for a 9-year-old, or maybe even smaller than the other kids their age.

But with travel teams, it always seems that it's the bigger kids who are the ones who dominate the action. Why? Because the physically more developed children can literally push around the average-sized kids easily. Indeed, the other kids are often somewhat intimidated by the larger children. As a result, the average or below-average-sized kids tend to shy away from the action, in fear of being pushed around or knocked to the ground.

Let me illustrate. Every year around the middle of August, the Little League World Series is held in Williamsport, PA. Every year, the teams that tend to advance to the finals are those teams that have at least one or two huge 12-year-olds on their team. It's not uncommon for these kids to stand 5'10" and weigh 180 lbs. and be only 12!

Now, ask yourself. Are you surprised that these big kids usually dominate all the pitching and the hitting in these games? Of course not. After all, they're competing against average-sized 11- and 12-year-olds. But if there's one rule you must never forget, it's that everything changes in sports once kids go through adolescence. We'll come back to this reality later on in the book, but if your child is under the age of 10, don't panic too soon about their size (or lack thereof).

Practice, Practice, and More Practice

Do you recall the old joke about the tourist in New York City who stops a man who's carrying a violin case? The tourist, eager to see all the famous spots in the city, asks simply: "How do I get to Carnegie Hall?"

The violinist responds simply: "Practice, practice, and more practice."

There's no question that one becomes proficient in a sport by practicing and eventually mastering certain athletic skills. Assuming that your child has a certain level of athletic ability, then the real key to improvement in athletics is by constant repetition of skills.

This is hardly a secret, but it still bears emphasizing here. Let's put it this way. You have two 10-year-olds. Both enjoy playing basketball, and they both play on teams. One youngster goes to basketball practice once a week, and then plays in the game on Sundays. During practice, as part of the drills, he'll shoot 10 or 15 free throws. Sometimes, in the games, he'll get fouled, and he'll get the opportunity to shoot one or two free throws a game.

Meanwhile, the other 10-year-old also goes to practice once a week, and then plays in a game on Sundays. And like his friend, he'll shoot 10 or 15 free throws in practice and a couple more in the game. But on the other days of the week, when there's no official team practice, this 10-year-old will go outside to a basketball court and practice shooting free throws by himself for an hour or two. He's done this all season.

Now, here's the ultimate question: which one of these two 10-year-olds do you think will become more proficient at shooting free throws? The answer is obvious. As a sports parent, if you want your child to become better at their sport, the key still persists in *their* desire to want to get better. And parental praise—not parental prodding—is still the main ingredient to making this happen. A little sincere parental praise—"You know, John, you're really making tremendous progress with your free-throw shooting"—goes a long, long way in nourishing your child's inner drive.

So, to me, the real question here is not so much about getting a kid on a travel team at a young age, but rather getting your youngster to maintain the inner desire to want to practice his or her skills on their own. Common sense? Perhaps. But if pressed, I think every sports parent would agree that **the key to athletic proficiency for any youngster is practice, practice, and more practice.**

Every young basketball player has the dream of being able to dribble the ball with either hand. Every young soccer player has the dream of being able to kick the ball hard with either foot. Every young baseball player has the dream of being able to hit line drive after line drive. But if one wants to truly develop their skills and become proficient in a sport, pure God-given athletic talent will only take them so far. Eventually, only those who know how to practice on their own will become the stars.

Here's the formula:

Talent + Parental Praise + Practice + Practice = Stardom

Unfortunately, kids today have a lot more distractions than we did as kids. How many times have you heard one of your parenting colleagues note, "You know, when we were kids, we would play ball on the playground from sun-up to sundown. We only quit when it got too dark to play, or when we were called in for dinner."

Yes, those were the good ol' days. But those days are gone. Our children have lots of activities and distractions vying for their attention, and many of these modern-day distractions quite simply did not exist when we were growing up: cable TV, video games, the Internet, cell phones, extreme games, and so on. Chances are that if we had these same distractions when we were kids, we would have rarely played ball from sunrise to sunset.

But no matter. The reality today is that kids will only continue to play sports if they have fun playing them. And kids today only have fun in a sport if they feel that they are either competent at it, or that they are becoming more competent at it. We live in an era of instant gratification. Young athletes today simply do not have the patience to keep playing a sport unless they experience a certain amount of instant gratification. After all, they can always find instant gratification from video games, skateboarding, or other nontraditional sports, and quite honestly, that's what a lot of young athletes eventually turn to.

This is why parental praise is so important to a kid's development. As a sports parent, you have to learn the right process to give your child the right kind of positive feedback. This can be a little tricky as the child gets a little older, and you feel compelled to provide some constructive criticism. To accomplish both purposes, you need to learn how to prepare and deliver a *praise sandwich*.

How to Give a Praise Sandwich

Here's the irony of today's talented athletes: You have to understand that young kids feel that they only have to practice their sport once or twice a week during an organized session, and then play a game or two on the weekend. That's it. And if they are naturally proficient at the sport, then there's no inherent drive, or motivation, to push them to keep practicing and improving their skills. As a result, you might encounter this typical conversation:

You: "Sweetheart, do you want to go out with Dad and kick the soccer ball around?"

8-Year-Old: "I don't think so. . . . I mean, I just scored two goals in the game last week. Why do I need to go out and practice?"

Of course, as an adult, you know exactly why she might need to practice some more. But from your child's perspective, she feels that she's already on top of her game—so why does she have to go through the effort of an unwanted practice session, when she can just plop down in front of the TV and watch videos?

As a sports parent, your child's lack of enthusiasm can be very frustrating. But you're going to have to be very delicate in how you handle it. On one hand, if you absolutely insist that your little one go out and practice with you, then it won't be long until she develops an extreme distaste for the sport—and for you. Kids don't like being bossed around, and they certainly don't want to feel obligated to have to practice a sport that they're supposed to enjoy.

Yet you may also feel that your child really does need to develop some key skills. For example, it's clear that your daughter is a talented little basketball player. But it's also clear that she needs to work on her ball-handling skills; right now, she dribbles the ball only with her right hand. You know that if she wants to become more proficient at handling the ball, the sooner she learns how to use her left hand, the better she'll become.

So how can you make your point in a subtle yet positive way? This is where the **praise sandwich** approach comes in handy. This involves giving your child two slices of positive feedback along with an inner slice of constructive criticism.

Let's work with the example of the young basketball player who dribbles only with her right hand. The first step is to find the right time and setting for a little chat. The best time is probably during a quiet time, perhaps right before bedtime for your youngster, or sometimes during a long car ride when it's just the two of you. But no matter when you have the conversation, you have to start the discussion with that first slice of praise:

First Slice of Praise: "You know, Joanna, you really have developed an amazing ability to bring the ball up the court, and to shoot it. You're developing nicely into quite a solid offensive player for your team." (This first slice of praise should solidly let the youngster know that you openly and proudly recognize that she has talent on the basketball court. This is absolutely essential because all kids love praise. Better yet, they **respond** to praise.)

Slice of Constructive Criticism: "And you know what? If you could ever develop the ability to dribble the ball with your left hand as well as you do with your right hand . . . well, that would be something very special." (Note that the criticism—that the young basketball player dribbles only with her right hand—is presented in such a way that you're not criticizing her, but rather giving her another pathway to make her game that much better. The constructive criticism has to be well thought-out before it's delivered. Otherwise, it could lose its impact, or even backfire.)

Second Slice of Praise: "And if you did develop the ability to dribble with either hand, well, I just don't know how any team could guard you when you bring the ball up to the front court. I mean, you'd be unstoppable!" (Again, a healthy dose of praise with the vague promise of even greater stardom on the basketball court. This will get her to start thinking about learning how to dribble with both hands, because it may mean even greater glory to herself and her game.)

Do praise sandwiches work? Well, don't be surprised if you see your little one working on her dribbling skills with either hand at the very next practice. And when you do, give her another big slice of praise.

Is this just a device to get one's child to practice more? Absolutely! Remember that the basis for a certain mastery of skills in any sport is constant and repetitive practice. And if a praise sandwich gets your child to put down the television remote control or to step aside from the computer and go outside to work on her dribbling skills, then you know that she (and you) are on the right track.

Practice against Your Child as a Peer, Not as a Parent

One of the interesting questions about parents practicing with their child is the concern as to whether you should compete against them as a grown-up, or at the skill level of someone their own age.

Example: Your 9-year-old challenges you to a game of HORSE in basketball. But like most 9-year-olds, the best he can do is perhaps make a lay-up, or maybe even shoot the ball up at the hoop from 8 feet away. As the parent, do you compete against your child in the game as an adult; or do you compete against them as though you were an over-sized 9-year-old yourself?

Answer: For kids that young, you're only going to discourage them if you compete against them as an adult. Obviously, it's not fair that you're fully grown and have the ability to shoot the ball from a variety of spots on the court. If you insist on doing this, it won't be too long before your youngster loses interest in playing against you. Why? Because they'll realize quickly that they have no chance in defeating you.

"But that's okay," I can hear some parents protesting, "The only way they'll get better is if they compete against better players." Well, maybe when they get to be a little older, such as in their early teenage years. But under the age of 10, they'll only become discouraged. Even young kids recognize when they have no chance at winning in a competition, and when that happens, they quickly lose interest and will turn to some other activity.

What to do? Just pretend that you're the same age as your child, and try to compete as though you had the same ability level as your youngster. You can even tell them that you're going to try and compete as though you were someone their age, only a little bigger.

Should I Let My Child Win?

No, not necessarily. Simply compete at their level. That means you have to limit your ability to shoot the ball, and if you miss, well, then that's the way it goes. Ideally, if things go well, you will win some of the games of HORSE and your child will win some of the games, too. That's the best possible outcome.

But letting them win easily serves no purpose at all. Again, kids are pretty smart. They'll quickly pick up on the fact that you're letting them prevail. And once that happens, they'll realize there's no challenge or fun in doing that either. Once again, they'll quickly lose interest.

Dealing with Disappointment

You know the scene. Your little one's team has just lost a game; perhaps it's their first loss of the season. And as the game comes to an end, the kids on the team, including yours, burst into tears that roll down their faces.

For any parent, this is always a heartbreaking sight. But as an adult, you also know that in sports, for every winning team, there's also a losing team. That's just the natural balance of team sports. Unfortunately, the recognition of that reality doesn't reduce the inner pain you feel for your child as they come off the field in tears.

Well, the good news in all of this is that children under the age of 10 have a remarkable resiliency to bounce back quickly from a defeat or a setback. Within a matter of seconds, usually, the tears will stop and they will look around and wonder what the next activity of the day is. Of course, the bad news is that, sometimes, the parents have a much more difficult time dealing with the emotional letdown of a loss than their child does.

While it's okay to feel disappointed too, please don't let your dismay linger too long. Indeed, it's now your job to give that sincere pat on the back and praise to your son or daughter. **It's your job to make them feel better—not for them to make you feel better.**

Especially in the case of those youngsters for whom sports is a big deal, the way you as the parent handle defeat is a key lesson for them—not only in terms of exhibiting proper sportsmanship, but also in not letting their self-confidence waver. After a loss, especially a tough loss, you have to become a big-time cheerleader. That means you have to be there to offer unconditional positive support for your child. And be ready to point out the specific plays in the game that they did well.

And along these lines, as with most things in life, timing is everything. It's best to offer your support right after the game.

Avoid the Post-Game Analysis

One of the surest ways to alienate your youngster away from sports is to try and engage them in a detailed Post-Game Analysis (PGA). This usually occurs in the family station wagon or minivan just as the game has ended, and your young athlete has climbed into the car on their way to their next event or game of the day.

As a caring parent who wants only the best for their child, you will be tempted to quickly delve into a critique of the game they just played in.

You might say something like, "Gee, Michael, you had an open net to score that goal late in the first half . . ." or "Sarah, how come the coach took you out of the game in the third inning?" or "Tommy, did you lose that pop-up in the sun . . . or did you just miss it?"

All of these questions and comments certainly seem innocent enough—at least from an adult's perspective. But for a kid, these kinds of queries seem like you're putting them under a hot spotlight and grilling them.

"But I'm just trying to go over some of my son's miscues on the field while they're still fresh in his mind," many Moms and Dads will note. "Besides, if I don't go over the mistakes with them, who will?"

Good sentiment. Poor execution.

The last kind of interaction you want to have with your athlete right after a game is to ask them about some of the mistakes they made. You may be very tempted to go over their errors, but this is definitely not the right time to do it. In fact, this is the precise time to do just the opposite. If you feel compelled to go over the game with your child, talk to them about all the great plays they made during the game—not the poor ones!

Let your child bask in the glory of having played well. Believe me, there's plenty of time to go over those aspects of their game that need to be corrected. Again, the best and most effective way to offer constructive criticism to young athletes is with a praise sandwich. And praise sandwiches should be delivered several hours after the game is over.

Why the concern over too much exposure to a PGA? Because if you continue to cross-examine your child after each and every game, it won't take long for the youngster to figure out that he had better play well all the time; otherwise, he's in for a long and painful lecture with Mom or Dad. And when the child comes to that realization, it's not long before they either ask you to not come to their games any more, or worse yet, they tell you that they no longer want to play the sport.

Sound drastic? Yes it does. The cruel irony is that this kind of PGA-induced burnout occurs only because the parent was merely eager to go over their kid's mistakes right after the game in order to help them improve. In effect, the parent only meant well. But they are "rewarded" with their athletic child turning away from their sport.

Individual Sports vs. Team Sports

So far, I have mostly focused on traditional team sports, such as soccer, basketball, and the like. Of course, there are many competitive sports that focus on an individual performer. Those sports include swimming, gymnastics, figure skating, golf, tennis, track and field, and several others.

Do the same rules apply here regarding the right age to get started?

For the most part, yes. It's acknowledged that for some individual sports, a youngster will often reach their peak performing years as early as their mid-to-late teens. As a result, it's essential that they be exposed to their sport early on. The tricky part, of course, is twofold: how do you know which sport your child is going to excel in, and if they do start early, how do you keep them interested?

Which sport? First off, it's absolutely essential that your child discover the sport that they naturally enjoy. If you force your kid to be a tennis player, simply because you and your spouse enjoy tennis, then don't be surprised if your child quickly burns out. As a concerned parent, let your 5- or 6-year-old experiment with various sports. If they eventually find one they truly like, then you can gradually allow them to play more and more of that sport. Again, **it's essential that they build a true passion for their sport**; otherwise, they'll drop it as they get older.

Once you're convinced that they do have a growing love for the sport, then you can ask your child if they would like to take lessons. Remember—never force anything on the youngster. Ask them if they would like to pursue it. From there, you can gently introduce some coaching, but again, don't overdo it. Use parental common sense, and of course, parental praise.

Also, don't be reluctant to let your child play other sports as well, even as they focus more and more on their favorite. As one 9-year-old told me, "I play tennis seriously . . . but I play soccer and basketball and other sports, too." His meaning was that while he's actively focusing more and more on his tennis, he also has the freedom to enjoy other sports. For those youngsters who are clearly drawn to one individual sport, it's never a bad idea to let them balance that with participation on some team sports as well. After all, lots of things change in life—and his or her interest in one sport may change dramatically in the years to come.

THE LEGACY OF EAST GERMANY'S ATTEMPT TO PRODUCE SUPERIOR ATHLETES

Back in the 1970s, the East German government became world renowned for enacting an extraordinarily effective program of pushing—and developing—its young children into becoming top Olympic athletes. The East German government, which was Communist, felt that there was no better way to tell the rest of the world how superior their country was than by producing the greatest athletes of their time.

And indeed, they were quite successful. During its relatively brief lifetime as a separate nation, East German athletes won more Olympic medals per capita than any other country of significant size. That's the good news.

The bad news was that behind the East German borders, young athletes were being exposed to all sorts of horrible personal sacrifices, both emotionally and physically, at very young ages in order to meet the government's demand for developing the most promising athletes.

Children as young as 5 and 6 were handpicked by East German officials from all over the country simply because these youngsters seemed to exhibit some sort of athletic ability. During the 1970s, more than 12,000 East German youngsters were shipped off to special athletic facilities, where they lived in dorms away from their homes and families. Their days were spent working on a particular sport (each child was chosen to specialize in only one athletic endeavor) and, when time allowed, they received some schooling as well. The children's diets were monitored very carefully, and in many cases they were ordered to take certain pills or medications. The kids were told simply that these pills would help them improve in their sports.

The truth, we now know, was that these young East German athletes—male and female—were given all sorts of steroids and other illegal muscle-enhancing drugs to make them stronger, faster, and better than their Olympic opponents. And the steroids in particular had the kind of immediate impact that the East German coaches wanted: their athletes were bigger and stronger than everyone else in the world, and lots of Olympic medals were won.

Unfortunately, as drug testing became more sophisticated, these East German athletes were eventually caught, banned from future Olympics, and stripped of their medals. In fact, in some cases where young females had consumed steroids for years, their actual gender was brought into question by the Olympic judges. Several East German female athletes had developed distinctively male characteristics, including facial hair and high levels of testosterone, which left them sterile.

Even worse, many of these young female East German athletes who were forced to ingest drugs ultimately had to endure terrible lifelong side effects, including premature death and serious birth defects in their children.

It's now acknowledged by all sports medical experts that the East Germans, in their zeal to win Olympic medals at all costs, went far beyond the limits of what is both acceptable and healthy in the development of talented athletes. For decades, the East Germans have been disgraced, not only at the way in which they ruined the lives of many of their athletes, but also in the way that they attempted to cheat in the Olympics.

Today, ironically, the German government is once again trying to rebuild a world-class system of athletics. And, as you might expect, there are several notable similarities to their current program as compared to how the East Germans used to run their athletic development programs back in the 1970s.

For starters, the Germans still scour the countryside looking for talented young athletes. In the reunited Germany, the government is now spending close to a billion dollars to help promote top competitive athletics. There are now close to 90,000 sports clubs throughout Germany where young athletes compete. The standout athletes from these clubs are then encouraged to transfer from their regular school into a school where sports are heavily emphasized. This all happens when the athletes are very young. For promising gymnasts, for example, this transfer of schools can occur as early as the third grade. For other sports, such as rowing or weight lifting, it may not happen until the child is in 9th or 10th grade. But regardless of the age when they begin to specialize in a sport, it's clear that their career in athletics quickly becomes the top focus in their young lives.

Does the new German system work? Well, by most accounts, yes it does. Germany won more medals than any other country at the 2002 Winter Olympic Games in Salt Lake City. Are other nations concerned about this sudden turnaround? Says Mike Moran, a spokesman for the United States Olympic Committee: "There's no question that there has been a dramatic increase by the Germans. But as proud as the Germans may be of what they did in Salt Lake, we [the USOC] were only one medal behind them."

However, the USOC has no plans to change its current style of developing athletes. As you may know, unlike most countries where Olympic athletes have their training regimens funded by the government, American Olympians are funded only by private donations from private citizens and the corporate world.

How long can the U.S. keep this policy and maintain its competitive edge in athletics? No one knows, but one trend is clear: other nations have taken note of Germany's program and their quick success, and these other countries are now beginning to institute similar athletic training programs for their kids. Along those lines, the most recent nation to adopt a talent identification program is Australia.

What happens to all of these talented athletes, who have focused so much of their young lives on one sport, when they are forced to finally retire from competition? That's a very important question that, unfortunately, very few countries or their coaches have yet to sit down and study or answer responsibly. Yet it's a question that begs a serious response. (*New York Times*, Sept. 10, 2002)

CHAPTER TWO:
The Question of Specialization

"My 10-year-old daughter is very good at soccer, basketball, softball, tennis . . . for that matter, whatever sport she tries, she seems to get the hang of it quickly. But her tennis instructor has told me that if she starts to specialize in tennis and only tennis, then she's got a good chance to become terrific—maybe even get a college scholarship. As a parent, what do I do?"

"My son, who's a freshman in high school, grew up playing soccer in the fall, basketball in the winter, and baseball in the spring. But now the high school soccer coach is pressuring him to give up basketball and baseball. The coach has said to my son, 'Look, you're not that good in either baseball or basketball to ever play pro or earn a scholarship. But in soccer, if you just focus on that sport, you might get a shot.' As a parent, what do I advise my son?"

The question of specialization is one of the very first issues parents today have to confront regarding their son or daughter in the world of competitive sports. But what surprises Moms and Dads the most is how this decision is usually forced upon them when their child is as young as 9 or 10 years old. And for most parents who want only the best in sports for their child, this can be a most difficult decision. After all, at such a young age, who knows what sport their child is going to be the best at, or for that matter, what sport they will enjoy the most as they get older.

Curiously, some parents don't give this decision a second thought. They may have always wanted their son or daughter to play a specific sport—perhaps a sport that they themselves played as a child. As such, they can't wait to get their child to specialize in the sport that they loved. From this parenting perspective, the child ought to play tennis (or golf, or whatever) "seriously," and to play that one singular sport all year round. And, in the off-season, the child can just "fool around" with sports like basketball, football, or hockey.

For these adults, there is evidence that their decision makes sense. After all, sports like golf and tennis can be played for years to come, while with sports such as football or baseball or soccer, for the most part, one's playing career is over at the end of high school or college. And quite honestly, in some parents' estimation, having their child learn how to play an individual sport at such a young age will allow them to perhaps become more competitive in that sport as they reach the junior high school and high school levels.

But remember: there is no scientific data that proves starting a child early in a sport is going to guarantee their future success. Parents often point to Tiger Woods as "Exhibit A" of how an early introduction to a sport—in his case, golf—can help propel an athlete to stardom. But Earl Woods, Tiger's dad, has made it abundantly clear that he never pushed Tiger or forced the game onto him. It was always up to Tiger—not his dad—to decide if he wanted to go out and practice. As a former top-flight athlete himself (collegiate baseball), Earl knew instinctively that it was important for Tiger to find the drive within himself.

Ultimately, no matter how much a youngster is pushed into a sport, there is the key element of pure physical talent to consider. Going back to the example of Tiger Woods, it's clear that he could have been an outstanding athlete in any sport he chose. He just happened to choose golf. Moms and Dads, always remember this: **Athletic talent is simply God-given; it cannot be taught, learned, or forced onto a youngster, no matter how much a parent may try.**

Tiger Woods started—and starred—at an early age. He specialized in golf by the time he was 3 or 4. And of course, this early start in his sport worked for him. But there are plenty of well-known athletes who did not specialize in just one sport as a kid. For example, most sports fans know Deion Sanders as one of the greatest professional football and baseball players of his day. But did you know that Deion was also an All-State basketball player in high school in Florida? In other words, he kept playing different sports right through high school, college, and into the pro ranks. Deion saw no reason to specialize in one sport, and it certainly didn't hurt his career.

Bo Jackson was another two-sport superstar, having played football and baseball in college and then professionally for the Oakland Raiders and Kansas City Royals. Then there's Jackie Joyner-Kersee, the great Olympic track star. People often forget that Jackie was a star basketball player at UCLA. Larry Walker, the great slugger for the Colorado Rockies, started out as a hockey goalie with dreams of playing in the National Hockey League. The same was true of Tom Glavine, the longtime All-Star major league pitcher. Glavine, who's from Massachusetts, was drafted out of high school by the Los Angeles Kings of the National Hockey League. And you might remember that Chris Drury, who has grown up to be a star NHL goal scorer, also led the Trumbull, Connecticut, Little League team to the World Championship at Williamsport, Pennsylvania, a few years back.

What does all this mean?

Simply that if your child is a gifted athlete—and I mean truly gifted—then ultimately he or she will not be forced to make a choice about specializing in a sport at an early age unless they want to. And for most athletically inclined kids, they're most likely not going to want to choose one sport over another.

Everybody knows Yogi Berra, the great Hall of Fame catcher for the New York Yankees. When Yogi had to counsel his own children about specializing or not, Yogi simply told them to play what they wanted to play. Remembers Dale Berra, one of Yogi's sons who went on to play for ten years as a major league infielder for the Pittsburgh Pirates and the Yankees, "I used to love all sports as a kid, and I mean, all sports. I played football in the fall, hockey in the winter, and then baseball in the spring and summer. I never specialized in just one sport, and I guess, looking back, it never hurt my development." Indeed, lots of professional athletes today share Dale Berra's views and experience.

So What's the Right Pathway?

As you might imagine, there is no singular "right" answer to this question. So much depends upon the individual child and his or her passion for sports and competition, as well as upon their own instinctive drive to want to excel in sports. As such, the only "right" pathway is to allow your child the freedom to develop a passion for a sport (or sports) so that they will want to practice their skills on their own and also try to reach their full athletic potential— whatever that potential may be.

Funny thing. In the North American culture of sports, reaching one's potential is seen as climbing a kind of pyramid in order to reach the peak of one's ability. It's almost as though one should constantly strive to reach that peak, and once there, do one's best to refine one's skills so that one can stay at one's "peak performance" for a long, long time.

But the basic assumption in all this is that there's a finite peak of potential that an athlete can reach; that is, that there's a real limit as to how good an athlete can become. In contrast, in Japan, there's no such conception as reaching one's peak potential. In the Japanese athletic mindset, one can always keep working to push one's potential even further. There is no sense of "one's potential" being finite or limited. As a result, even the top athletes in Japan are constantly pushing themselves to reach beyond, even when their theoretical "peak" years of athletic performance are long behind them.

One example of this mindset is the great Japanese baseball slugger Sadaharu Oh. Oh, who hit 868 home runs in his professional Japanese career, was often praised as he reached his later years as a player because he was always working to improve his home run batting stroke. When asked why he worked so hard, Oh replied: "Because I want to keep getting better."

But in North America, and for that matter, in the rest of the world's athletic culture, there's a very strong sense that an athlete's time clock is always ticking. And that clock starts ticking when the athlete is very young. It's almost as though the individual has only so many years to first learn their sport, then play it and practice it, and of course, play it well enough to advance to higher levels.

More specifically, if a child first picks up a baseball bat or kicks a soccer ball at age 4 or 5, then they have until they're 18 to become extremely talented at their sport. If they're good enough by age 18, then they'll be able to perhaps compete for a spot on a college team. But of course, even if they're good enough to play college ball, they'll most likely be finished at the age of 21 or 22.

You can do the math. That's a stretch of only 17 years—from age 5 to age 22. And that's only if they're good enough to play college sports. For the vast majority, the farthest they'll ever go in organized sports is through their senior year in high school—or age 18. That's a run of only 13 years—from age 5 to 18. After that, for the vast majority of youngsters, their competitive athletic career is finished.

Because of this unspoken reality, many parents feel it's absolutely essential to have their athlete focus on one sport as young as possible. It's almost as though they feel that the youngster is "wasting their time" playing other sports when they could be concentrating on just that one sport— the sport that might propel him or her to a potential college scholarship or professional career.

And with some individualized sports, such as tennis, swimming, gymnastics, and figure skating, it is somewhat imperative that a youngster begins concentrating on that sport at an early age. Why? Because in those competitive individualized sports, the peak performing years tend to skew toward one's late teens, which is much younger than many of the traditional team sports.

"But How Do I Know if My Child Is Going to Be a Star?"

Good question. Let's work with one of the more competitive sports: figure skating. Assume that your child takes to ice skates quite naturally, and as early as age 5 or 6 it's clear that she's quite mobile and fluid on the ice. Then, by the time she reaches 8 or 9, she's already entered into some local figure skating competitions and done very well. In fact, lots of other parents are coming up to you and congratulating you and your daughter, telling you that "she's a real natural" and that "I'll expect to see her competing in the next Winter Olympics."

Of course, all of this makes you and your daughter feel proud and quite good about yourselves. After all, it's a wonderful feeling to compete, do well, and then relish all of the positive attention that's showered on you.

But now, as your child reaches her 10th or 11th birthday, it's becoming increasingly clear to you that if she really does want to take the next step forward in her figure skating career, then you have to start thinking about making a much more serious commitment to the sport. Commitment, in this case, usually means hiring a professional skating coach, getting lots and lots of practice time in a rink (which over the course of time can cost thousands of dollars), spend even more money on traveling to the various venues for competitions, and on and on. Also, there's less time for the child's schoolwork and extracurricular activities, not to mention her friendships with classmates. In other words, stepping up her involvement is a major commitment in every sense of the word and, of course, there's never any guarantee that your child is going to become one of the stronger skaters as she develops through her teenage years.

So how does a parent decide to make this commitment? From one point of view, if you don't allow your child to pursue her dream of becoming the next Sarah Hughes or Nancy Kerrigan, then she and you may go through the rest of your lives wondering whether she could have been good enough to become an Olympic skater. On the other hand, if you do decide to take the plunge and devote your child's life to figure skating for the foreseeable future, then you have to wonder just how much of her childhood are you really going to sacrifice for skating.

By the way, speaking of Sarah Hughes, you might want to take note that her mother and father did their very best to allow Sarah to maintain a solid balance between her skating career and her normal school life. Rather than move out of her home on Long Island, New York, in order to train with coaches in various parts of the country, Sarah stayed home. She went to school every day, found a rink fairly close by where she could practice long hours, and also had the chance to maintain a so-called normal childhood. And since she won an Olympic gold medal, one would have to say that her parents took a very sensible and successful approach.

A Quick Set of Guidelines for Individual Sport Athletes

But even so, how can you make up your mind about committing your child to skating, or tennis, or swimming, or gymnastics, or any sport that demands tremendous hours of practice as a youngster? Here's what I recommend as some basic guidelines:

1. Seek out an objective analysis of your child's abilities. To do this, rather than simply listen to the compliments and praise of your youngster's current coach, go out and solicit the opinions of at least two or three other experienced coaches. Let these coaches watch your child perform independently and then let them give you a candid idea of what they think your child's chances are to develop into a top competitor.

2. Don't rush into making a snap or emotional decision. Listen to what the coaches are saying about your child's abilities. Ask them as many questions as you can. Do not be defensive if they tell you that they think your child is very, very good, but not quite good enough, in their opinion,

to become a real star. And if you hear a similar opinion expressed by more than one coach, try to think seriously about what is going to be best for your child's overall development as well as athletic development.

3. Sit down and talk with your youngster. Get them to talk to you about their feelings regarding their sport, and gauge just what their passion or desires are in relation to their future dreams. **If it's clear to you that they have an absolutely insatiable desire to be the best, no matter what it takes, then take that seriously.** Never count out a child's drive to become the very best they can be.

On the other hand, if you get the sense that they sometimes don't mind missing practice, or wish they could have more play dates with their friends, or feel that they are missing out on their teenage friendships, then take this seriously as well. In their own youthful way, they may be giving you every hint of what their real feelings are regarding their sport.

4. As you know, you are never going to get a clear-cut right or wrong decision on this. It's just too difficult to sort through all the emotions. But the more objective and independent your analysis is, and the more you can communicate honestly with your youngster, the better chance you and your child have of making the best decision. As a dedicated and concerned sports parent, that's all you can ask for.

"My Child Plays One Sport Seriously, and Others Just for Fun. . . ."

I often hear this distinction made by parents of kids who have decided to specialize in one sport. Trying to have the best of both worlds, even the child will tell me, "I play tennis seriously, but I play soccer and basketball just for fun. . . ."

What he means is that he spends hours and hours hitting a tennis ball, and he competes in that sport with every bit of intensity that he can muster at a young age. But if he just wants to have fun with buddies, he'll hack around with a basketball or a soccer ball.

Please note that the key word here is **fun**. I'm always a little wary of the 9-year-old who tells me that he plays other sports just for fun, while he takes tennis seriously. That has always signaled to me a major concern regarding the potential of burnout from their "serious" sport. After all, if the basic attraction of the sport is not to have fun—but to take it seriously—then you have to wonder just how long even the most dedicated young athlete can keep pushing himself to compete and win. Never discount the "fun" element in the attraction of a sport.

Unfortunately, there are no reliable statistics available regarding burnout of youngsters in a particular sport, but I would guess that a good percentage of them are youngsters who specialized in one sport—and who played that sport **seriously**—at a very young age. In contrast, I think it's rare to find a youngster who did not specialize in a sport—who played lots of sports growing up—who ever felt he or she was experiencing burnout. After all, for these kids, when one sport got a little tedious, they simply played something else.

In conclusion, there are no hard and fast rules regarding specialization. But if a youngster is truly an all-around natural athlete, a parent should not fear that they're making a mistake if they do not have the kid specialize. And if, on the other hand, you feel your child really needs to specialize in a sport if they are going to have a chance to progress to higher levels of competition, then perhaps that's something you really ought to consider.

CHAPTER THREE:
The Middle School Years

By the time your young athlete has reached middle school, and that would include ages 11, 12, and13, it should be fairly clear to all observers that he or she has developed a solid interest in sports.

This is not to suggest that a youngster may not be drawn to athletics at a later age; indeed, some are, and especially those who experience late growth spurts in adolescence. But for the vast majority of kids, after having been exposed to sports since they were younger, they now find athletic competition to be a source of great fun and heightened self-confidence. For many, sports is also the way in which they develop social contacts, make new friends, and in general, develop a central peg on which to hang the rest of their young lives.

This is all to the good. While we as grown-ups know that very few young athletes ever go on to a lengthy career based upon their God-given athletic skills, for kids in middle school, they are still living their athletic dreams. They still hope that they'll be the one to score the winning touchdown in the big game, or to make the game-ending basket, or to outswim all of their competitors to win the gold medal.

But of all the developmental ages in sports, the middle school years are usually most pivotal in helping determine just how good, and how far, the young athlete will go in their sports career. Why? Because as the child continues to grow, not only physically but emotionally as well, their close-knit world of athletic reality will begin to expand rapidly. And as it does, their perception of sports, and of their own involvement in sports, will be challenged for the first time. What this means is that as the child goes through elementary school, he or she usually gauges just how well they measure up against their athletic peers. But as they enter in the middle school years, they start to play kids and teams from other towns and school districts. This introduction of new and unknown athletic competition rapidly forces the young athlete to look beyond their own comfortable town borders. In short, they get their first taste of the "athletic real world."

Ages 10–11: Egocentric Worlds, Expanding Horizons, Practice for Fun

Most young athletes at this age are in the process of leaving elementary school and entering the middle school in their school district. From a parental perspective, bear in mind that your child is leaving the cozy confines of elementary school, and is now being ushered into a larger school with new teachers, and many times, new faces. Among those new faces will include new athletic peers as well, and that's significant.

Remember that most kids, and especially athletic children, see the world through thoroughly egocentric glasses. They can't wait to do well on the sport fields. Indeed, as 8 or 9 year olds, they'll try to score as many goals as they can. And the truth is, in most cases, they would always rather score themselves than pass to an open teammate, and so they can't wait to show their stuff when the opportunity is provided to them. This is not to indict young children; rather, this is to simply understand their point of perspective.

But when a youngster gets a little older, they gradually become aware that there are other athletes in their expanding world. And these athletes also seem to have many of the same athletic abilities that they have. This sudden realization—that athletic talent can be everywhere—is normal and fine; it's all part of the process of growing up in sports.

As a sports parent, sometimes you have to remind yourself of what really goes on inside a 10-year-old's head. At that age, they still love to get that shiny new uniform. They still get a big kick out of seeing their name on the back of their game jersey, or stitched into their travel jacket. When they go on road trips with their team, they certainly enjoy playing in the games, but they also seem to gain as much pleasure from playing video games or just hanging out with their teammates. As an adult, you have to understand that "away from the game" activity is vitally important to their enjoyment of their sports experience. Quite frankly, it's a major part of their socialization process as well.

What do you want your child to take away from all of this? Of course, a sense of fun and enjoyment is paramount. Why? Because if your athlete has a really good time participating in athletics, there's every expectation that they will want to continue playing sports in the years to come. Even better, if they truly have a knack for their sport, then there's a good chance they will go out and begin to practice on their own during their off hours. And as you know, the more they practice, the better they become.

Ages 12–13: Adolescence, Adversity, Specialization

As your child becomes a pre-teenager, some fundamentally important changes begin to occur in their lives. One of the most striking is the physical onset of adolescence. As all parents know, all sorts of amazing changes take place when our children reach their teenage years. But just as significantly, there are other key developments as well. For example, often at this age, kids are introduced to "tryouts" for school teams. This, of course, implies that there are real cuts made on sports teams at this level. For many young athletes, for the first time in their lives, they will face head-on the threatening reality of athletic adversity. How these kids handle these potential setbacks will have a major influence on the rest of their sporting careers.

At this age, there's also more pressure on kids to start to specialize in just one sport. Up until now, kids (along with their parents' help) were usually able to juggle as many sports as they wanted. But in the 7th or 8th grade, especially in those schools where multiple teams exist, it's incumbent upon the youngster to start making decisions. For example: softball and lacrosse are both spring sports—and you can't play on two school teams during the same season—so which one do you want to play? For many athletes, especially those who are gifted in a number of sports, this can be a very challenging decision to make.

What's the right answer? Of course, no one knows. But by the time your child is in 7th or 8th grade, you should set aside some time to have an honest discussion with him or her about what sport or sports they would like to pursue. Obviously, the best approach is for the youngster to tell you what they prefer. Ideally by this age, they already have a good idea of what they want to do. Sometimes, they may even surprise you with a very mature outlook, such as: "Well, I really love playing basketball with my friends, but I know that, deep down, I have a better chance of being successful in sports as a wrestler."

This kind of sports maturity often starts to show up in 8th graders. Remember this: kids today are not stupid, especially when it comes to judging their own merit and ability as an athlete. By the time they're 13, they have already been around long enough to see how they stack up against their athletic peers. They can see how physically big they are compared to the others, and how relatively strong they are, and how fast they are, and how skilled they are.

In much the same way that no one had to tell you how good (or how bad) you were in sports when you were in 8th grade, the same is true for kids today. Unlike the naïve 5th or 6th grader who had only themselves at the center of their own athletic world, by the time kids are finished with

8th grade, they have a whole new perspective on where they stand athletically in comparison to their peers.

Now, don't forget that there's another very important key factor in all of this: adolescence. **Just because a kid is the best or biggest athlete in 8th grade doesn't in any way guarantee that he's going to be the best or biggest when he's a junior or senior in high school.** The most obvious change that takes place during this time is one of physical growth. Lots of kids who are the tallest in 8th grade have, for the most part, reached their full adult height. Even though they may tower over the other 13-year-olds, they often stop growing after that. On the other hand, there are lots of other kids who keep growing and eventually catch up and, many times, end up growing much taller.

Other physical changes happen. Some kids who are chubby start to slim down. Others who are slow-footed become fast. Other kids who were weak-limbed start developing muscles. Especially with girls, many young athletes will simply seem to grow overnight when they're 12 or 13. Girls often are much taller than their male counterparts at this age. In fact, the sports pages are teeming with stories of late bloomers who became athletic stars near the end of their adolescence, not at the beginning. **Remember: it's still a matter of where you start, not where you finish—especially when adolescence is involved.**

To illustrate just how much physical size can change during the teenage years, let me relate an anecdote from my sports parenting colleague, Bob Bigelow. Bob, who was only of average height through middle school, grew up to be 6'8", an All-Ivy League basketball star, and a first round choice in the NBA draft. Here is Bob's story of a young and enthusiastic boys' basketball coach who had just been named head coach of the team at a small high school in Maine.

As the young coach walked through the hallways of the school, he was brimming with excitement for having landed the job. But his spirits really soared when he spotted two high school boys who were both at least 6'4"—and then there was another youngster who was 6'6".

"Wow!" the coach thought to himself. "Three kids with some real size—how lucky can I get?" With those thoughts in mind, the coach couldn't wait for the team's first practice. But when that day arrived, he looked at the kids who came out for the team and discovered that the tallest was no more than 5'11". There was no sign anywhere of the taller kids he'd seen earlier.

Confused, the coach took one of the senior players off to the side, and asked, "What about those three lanky kids I saw in the hallways? Don't they play hoops?"

Replied the senior: "Oh yeah, those guys used to play basketball back when we were in 7th and 8th grade. But they were actually shorter than the other kids then, and as a result, they got cut from the travel teams. So when they got cut, they just quit basketball."

The coach was incredulous. "But they would form a great front line for our team. . . ."

Said the senior, "Yeah, well, you know how adolescence is. Most of us on the team grew early on and we were the tall ones in middle school. Turns out we just stopped growing, and the other kids grew tall later on. Too bad they started to grow after they quit playing basketball."

The point of the story? Always remember that the adolescent years can change everything when it comes to kids and their size.

Here's another story about how everything can change during adolescence:

In the 2002 college football season, the leading running back for Princeton University was Cameron Atkinson. As of this writing, Cameron ranks fifth on the all-time Princeton career list as a running back. Not too shabby, considering Cameron stands only 5'7" and weighs 185 pounds. Even more impressive is that Cameron didn't start playing sports at all until he was in the ninth grade (he grew up and went to school in New Jersey, right outside Philadelphia and not far from Princeton).

Being such a great athlete, why didn't he compete when he was 8 or 10 or 12? Replies Cameron: "I was short and fat. I was just a pudgy kid who really didn't do much." As Cameron told the *New York Times*, he was too overweight to actively play on the peewee football team in his neighborhood. It was only when Cameron experienced a late growth spurt which spread his weight around more evenly that he decided to try out for football. (Of course, it wasn't as though Cameron did nothing while he was growing up. For starters, he spent his time hitting the books and became a top student. At Princeton, he's pre-med, majoring in chemistry, and is fluent in German.) (*New York Times*, Nov. 8, 2002)

But again, Cameron represents another example of a youngster who was hardly a star when he was a pre-teenager. It all came together for him athletically only after he started to grow during his adolescence.

What about Holding Your Child Back a Year in School?

Kendall Hayes is a longtime high school basketball coach in Potomac, Virginia, and he feels that he's a pretty good judge when it comes to pinpointing young and developing players. He's also more than aware that kids grow and physically mature at different rates and at different times during adolescence.

Coach Hayes knows this firsthand, because when he was a senior in high school—at age 18—he stood about 5'11". But as he went on to college, whereas most of his high school teammates had pretty much stopped growing, Kendall added another 6 or 7 inches to his frame. In short, he became the prototypical "late bloomer." As a senior in college, he was a full 6'6" tall.

Apparently, this late blooming runs in his family. Kendall's brother was another classic late bloomer. In his case, he finished high school at 5'7" and then grew another 6 inches during college as well. This lesson of late adolescent growth was not lost on Kendall. When his own son,

Eric, was in the 8th grade, it was clear to Coach Hayes that his son was quickly developing into a fairly talented basketball player. At the time, Eric was about 5'11"—fairly tall but not terribly unusual for a boy who's just about ready to start high school.

But for Coach Hayes, he wondered if his son would go through a similar late growth spurt like he and his brother did. "In my mind, I figured that if Eric had another extra year to grow in high school, then he might be good enough and tall enough to attract a number of college scholarships by the time he graduated."

The coach explained further: "Look, I'm a high school physical education teacher. I make a nice salary, but it's going to be tough to finance a college education for my son (Kendall and his wife have two daughters as well). If there is some way that my son can help pay for some of his college expenses with a basketball scholarship, then I'm all for it."

So what did Coach Hayes do? Hoping that Eric might also be a late bloomer, he decided to have Eric transfer from the local public school district into a parochial school. In doing this, it meant that Eric would have to repeat the eighth grade. But the sum effect was that he would now be a full year older than his new 8th grade classmates and teammates.

What about the social and academic repercussions for Eric? "It actually wasn't too bad a transition," observed his father. "Academically, Eric was actually able to take some new courses that weren't available in his old school, so he certainly wasn't bored by repeating 8th grade. And socially, since he was now involved in a new school, he just made new friends. So it worked out fairly well."

And of course, Eric is still playing basketball—and still growing. Only time will tell if that extra year of 8th grade will allow Eric to grow like his father and uncle did, and will propel him to become a top college prospect as a 19-year-old high school senior.

Is This Case Unusual?

Surprisingly, Eric's case really isn't that unusual at all. In the world of ice hockey, where physical size and strength are prized by college coaches and pro scouts, it's become almost routine for a normal 18-year-old high school senior to consider going off to prep school after finishing high school. For one, this extra year of schooling—known as doing a "post-graduate" year, or "PG" year for short—has traditionally allowed a hockey player with a so-so academic background to get an extra year to improve his grades for entrance into college.

But of course, the main benefit is that it allows an extra year of growth, weight training, and maturation for the young player. This is one reason why when you look at the roster of college hockey teams you often see that most of the players list their prep school as the last high school team they played for, even though they are 19 years old. In some cases, a player will even do two years of PG study in order to get better grades and, of course, to grow larger. Hence, it's not uncommon for a college freshman hockey player to be 19 or 20 years old.

There's a similar pattern with high school basketball players who want to go on to play college ball, but need to get their grades up. Here, the reason is not so much to allow the youngster to grow and mature another year—although that's a desirable side effect—but rather to give the youngster a chance to improve academic and SAT scores in order to qualify to play in the NCAA. Again, the bottom line is that you see more and more 19- and 20-year-olds listed as freshmen on college basketball teams.

What about Baseball Players?

In contrast to adding an extra year of development, professional baseball scouts are always looking for those prospects who are younger, not older. Ask any pro scout and he'll always tell you that he would much prefer to sign an 18-year-old rather than a 21-year-old. Why? Because with a teenager, the scout knows that the player will spend all of the next three years playing baseball every day, and will not be distracted by such things as school. Playing ball every day allows the youngster to speed up their baseball skills much more rapidly than playing ball in a college program. Remember, the NCAA is very strict about how many games a college team can play during the course of an academic year.

Let me clarify. A typical 18-year-old pro baseball player will spend 4-5 weeks in spring training, then be sent to a minor league team where he'll play a 140-game season, and when that's over, he'll be dispatched to an instructional league in the fall for another 5-6 weeks of daily baseball. He then might even go to a winter ball league during December and January. In other words, for most of the year, he's playing nonstop baseball.

For an 18-year-old college baseball player, he might play 4 weeks in the fall, then he'll break until February. Weather permitting, he'll play in the regular college season from February through early May. And then, perhaps, he'll play in a summer league two or three times a week. Obviously, even a serious college ballplayer will play a lot fewer games than a young pro.

Of course, the trade-off is that the professional ballplayer is gambling that he's going to make it to the major leagues some day. Bear in mind that recent statistics show that only about 15% of all minor leaguers ever get to the big leagues, even for just one day. In comparison, the college ballplayer can still hope to someday get signed to a pro contract, but along the way, he can finish his college degree so that just in case he's not the next Roger Clemens or Mike Piazza, he still has a college degree to fall back on.

In recent years, it's been brought to light that a number of players from the Caribbean countries have misrepresented their real age. Since birth certificates and record keeping have traditionally been a little lax in such countries as Cuba and the Dominican Republic, some pro ballplayers have said that they are only 21 or 22, when in fact, they are really 25 or

26, or even older. These discrepancies were recently brought to light, and in many cases, several major leaguers had their age jump two or three years overnight.

Why did these players lie about their age? Simple. They know that pro scouts like younger players, and so, if they could shave a year or two off their birth certificate, they knew such a move would not only improve their chances of getting signed, but would also help extend their careers as they got older.

But this is all changing. Because of the infamous Danny Almonte case (the Little Leaguer from the Bronx, New York, whose parents lied about his real age, saying he was 12 instead of 14), more and more pro scouts are becoming very exacting about seeing a ballplayer's actual birth certificate. And as baseball becomes more global, and kids from all over the world are signed to professional contracts, having official documentation of a player's real age will become essential.

What about Your Child?

Does all of the above mean to seriously suggest that you ought to hold your child back a year (or two) in order to maximize his or her athletic potential? That's a very personal decision that only you, as a parent and an adult, can make. No one has the right answer to this question.

But if you are considering the question, always bear in mind that athletics is only one small part of a kid's life. Other concerns must include the child's self-esteem (i.e. how will the child react to being left behind a year in school?); the child's social life (he or she will now be thrust into a group of new kids who are, for the most part, younger); and the child's academics (will your child be forced to repeat much of the same material in school that he or she learned last year?).

Again, there are no right or wrong answers here. But holding a child back in school—**specifically for the purpose of hoping to give them an**

edge athletically—is a pathway that seems to be laden with lots of potential emotional landmines. In other words, be very, very careful with your child's life when you are making decisions about their athletics.

THE FACTS ABOUT HUMAN GROWTH HORMONE

So what do you do if your son or daughter has not gone through a pre-teen growth spurt, or if they are relatively small for their age?

You may have heard of a substance called Human Growth Hormone (HGH). This hormone is sometimes prescribed by a pediatrician for a youngster whose pituitary gland is under-performing, most notably causing stunted growth. But while this pediatrician-driven prescription has been the customary usage of HGH, more and more parents of diminutive athletes are now asking doctors to prescribe HGH for their child so that they will add extra inches to their frame. And as you might imagine, it's not uncommon these days for doctors to provide this prescription for the child.

Indeed, according to a recent study reported in the *New York Times*, there is both good news and bad news regarding HGH. In this study, the effects from taking the medication are for real: people who took it gained lean body mass (mostly muscle) and lost body fat. And this occurred even when the subjects did very little in terms of working out. But on the downside, nearly half of those who took HGH developed serious problems with diabetes, aching joints, and swollen tissues. To quote the *New York Times*: "There is concern that growth hormone may have terrible long-term effects—in animals it can actually speed aging and reduce life span, and scientists fear it could promote the growth of cancers." (*New York Times*, Nov. 13, 2002)

So, should your son or daughter be allowed to take human growth hormone? Well, that depends on you and your physician—and of course, your child. Are there potential negative side effects from this kind of medication? Yes, there can be, and to that end you should always consult your physician about both the positives as well as the negatives of such an endeavor. Remember: you're talking about the long-term health and welfare of your child, so tread very carefully.

Travel Teams Vs. Middle School Teams

By the time your athlete reaches middle school, very often they are already playing on a travel team or teams. Because travel teams usually have extensive practice and game schedules, invariably there's the potential for all kinds of conflicts with the school-sanctioned team.

So what happens when there's a conflict between the two schedules? In particular, what happens when the school coach demands that every team member make it to all the practices and games—and the travel coach demands the same level of commitment? Regrettably, this is a very common problem.

Let me answer this question with a quick story. A few years ago, I was attending a coaches' conference in Florida. One of the seminars focused on the future of high school athletics in this country. From my perspective, as someone who graduated from high school in 1969 and played three varsity sports, the traditional system of high school sports seemed to work quite well. Kids entering the 9th grade would try out for the freshman or junior varsity team, and as they got older, they eventually made their way onto the varsity squad.

For me, as for millions of others, playing for one's local high school varsity team was the culmination of years of hard work and dedication. In effect, playing on the high school varsity team was the biggest sports accomplishment that an aspiring athlete could achieve.

Of course, back in the 1960s, 1970s and even 1980s, the concept of and access to travel teams was not as widespread as it is today. As a result, playing for one's high school team was often the only game in town. The high school coach ruled supreme; after all, there was no other place for talented athletes to play. But that all changed when travel teams began to catch on. These days, in communities all over the country, high school varsity coaches wonder each year if the best kids from the local travel team are going to play for the high school team. Why? Because since the travel teams are comprised mostly of the best athletes in the area, it seems the only attraction for a high school athlete to play for one's school team is simply because it affords them a chance to play with their school buddies. In terms of actual athletic competition, there's little question that the travel team plays at a much more competitive level than the high school team.

If you're a traditionalist like I am, this may all sound very foreign to you. But at that coaches' conference in Florida, I recall very vividly how two high school athletic directors from the Midwest predicted that **within a matter of 5–10 years, the vast majority of all high school varsity teams in this country will be relegated to the status of intramural squads.** Actually, they said that the only exception to this would be high school football, but for all the other sports where travel teams exist, it would be the rare youngster who would opt to play for their school's varsity team instead of a travel team.

I thought this was pure science fiction. But once I began to listen to these athletic directors talk about how travel teams had totally infiltrated their communities, and how the tradition of giving one's all for one's high school varsity team was quickly becoming extinct, I began to realize that perhaps this was not some way-off prediction, but a transition that is happening right now everywhere in the United States.

Think about it for a moment. You name the sport, and these days, there's some sort of travel program that's attracting the best and brightest young athletes away from their school teams. AAU basketball. USA Hockey. Junior Olympic Development in soccer. USTA tennis. And on and on. Furthermore, this trend is not going away; if anything—as the high school athletic directors predicted—it's a trend that's picking up speed.

Which Commitment Comes First?

So, to answer the original question, if there are conflicts, most top high school athletes will opt to play for their travel team rather than play for their high school team. **Again, if the purpose for the youngster is to play sports at the highest level and maybe attract some college recruiters. there's no question that the better way to do that is by playing on the travel squad.**

Again, speaking from personal experience, when our son John was growing up, he fell in love with skating and quickly became involved in ice hockey. He loved the speed of the sport and the excitement of scoring goals. As with most travel hockey teams, they played a very extensive schedule of games and practices, often going from September right through early March. During his middle school years, John played on travel teams but also found time to play on school teams as well. But by the time he got to high school, he was, in effect, given a choice by his high school hockey coach: you can still play on your travel team, but if there's a conflict, the high school team comes first.

Yes, there were conflicts. And yes, the travel team was vastly superior to any high school team in our area. But when I asked John what he wanted to do, he said: "Dad, there's no question that the travel team is much better competition than our high school team, but the travel team is composed of kids from all over the county. My high school team, on the other hand, are all of my buddies who I see everyday in class."

In other words, he still wanted to play travel, but he also cherished the fun of playing with his close friends. It's been my experience that many high school athletes will make the same kind of choice. That is, they want to have the best of both worlds.

But sometimes, that's not always possible. Bob Bigelow (not related to the basketball player mentioned earlier in this chapter) has been the head soccer coach of the Southside High School (Long Island, NY) girls' team for two decades. His teams have been consistently ranked not only number one in New York State, but number one in the nation. Just about all of the members of this high school team also play travel soccer. And for years, Bigelow balked at letting the girls play both travel and high school soccer at the same time. He wanted them to commit just to his high school program.

"But I found out right away that if the girls were forced to choose between the high school varsity team and their travel soccer team, ultimately I ended up the loser," Bigelow observed. "It didn't take me long to figure out that I had better start trying to schedule school games and practices so they wouldn't conflict with the travel games and showcases that the girls wanted to attend." This is a case where the high school coach had to become more flexible in his approach; otherwise he and his high school program would lose out.

JUST HOW TOUGH IS IT TO GET A COLLEGE SCHOLARSHIP?

Consider this: in the Washington, D.C. metro area, soccer has been a hot sport for years now. And at River Hills High School, coach Bill Stara is exceedingly proud that his boys' varsity team has won four state titles in seven years and has produced All-Met players in five of the last six years. That means, of course, that his team is chock full of top high school soccer players.

> But how many of these players have ever received a scholarship to play at a Division I school? Zero. "A pure soccer scholarship, they are few and far between," observes Stara. "You use soccer as a way to help get you into school. But if you are using it as a means to pay for school, my suggestion is you hire a tutor and get your kid an academic scholarship." (*The Washington Post*, Feb. 13, 2003)

What's the bottom line? Basically, you and your athlete will get your first taste of having to choose between a school team and a travel team during the middle school years. Many times, the middle school coach will be very flexible with a kid who plays on a travel team. But be forewarned: it's the rare high school coach who will allow a youngster to play for two teams at the same time. As a result, while your youngster is still in 7th or 8th grade, you might want to check out what the current high school policy is so that you can help prepare for a few years down the road.

Playing up a Grade in Middle School

"It's obvious to everyone—all the other parents as well as the kids— that our child happens to be physically a lot larger than the other kids his age. He's also—and I say this as objectively as I can—a lot more advanced athletically than the other kids his age. As such, we're thinking that maybe he ought to play up against older kids. . . ."

The statement above could have been uttered by many a parent of a middle school-aged athlete today.

It's an age-old question: should the bigger—and presumably more athletically dominant—youngster move up and play against older kids? The immediate reaction for many sports parents is that such a move is not only welcome, but a great honor: it's as though the rest of the sports community is acknowledging that this one particular boy or girl is a budding superstar.

There are also lots of sports parents who firmly believe that the more challenging the competition is, the better it is for their child. Even if their athlete is a little smaller and a bit weaker than the older kids, they feel it's going to pay off in the long run. That is, the 11-year-old who competes in a league of 12-year-olds is only going to benefit as he or she gets older.

For the most part, there's nothing wrong with having your child "play up" against older kids. (Please note that I'm going to limit this particular conversation to kids in the middle school grades. We'll return to the topic of kids playing up on the high school varsity level in the chapters on high school sports.) For starters, there can be something worthwhile in having your child step up their game to compete against kids who are older, bigger, stronger, faster, and more experienced. Kids who dominate in their own age bracket might find their sport a bit more daunting and challenging when placed in an older bracket. They might also find that they learn new skills from the older kids, skills that will only benefit their game.

Many top athletes today will tell you that they learned their craft as a kid by competing in the backyard against their older brothers or sisters. They may have been younger and presumably smaller, but in order to compete against their older siblings, these athletic kids had to accelerate their mastery of certain skills. In other words, these athletes were actually "playing up" against bigger kids, albeit against members of their own family in the backyard. Regardless, these top athletes today will tell you that they greatly benefited from this kind of superior competition.

Are there any downsides to "playing up"? Well, yes, there are a few issues. "Playing up" could actually backfire on you and your child. As a parent, ask yourself these tough questions:

• **Is my 10-year-old simply a very talented player for her age? Or does she totally dominate the competition to the point where the other coaches in the league are truly wary of her?**

There's a real difference here, and unless your child falls into that second category, you may not want to move your child up.

Why? Because if you accelerate your child into an older age bracket, and she is not ready for that kind of jump, she may begin to lose self-confidence in her game. Even worse, instead of accelerating her skill development, she may actually regress. She may look around, see that she's not only the youngest kid in the age bracket, but perhaps one of the smaller ones. Despite your sincere encouragement that she totally belongs in the advanced league, she may actually begin to withdraw from the competitive action and play very timidly. That, of course, would only serve to hinder, and not help, her development.

- **Will my 11-year-old son feel an added sense of pressure now that he's playing against 12-year-olds?**

Occasionally kids who dominate in their own age bracket get moved up to the next level and feel that they are obliged to dominate at that level as well. The problem is that they are no longer the "big fish in a small pond." Now they're just another fish, and a younger one against older kids, no less.

But you have to be careful that your 11-year-old doesn't have that sense of obligation to dominate. You have to sit down with them and explain that playing up against older kids will actually take the pressure off them. That is, because they're younger than the rest of the kids, there is no expectation at all for them to excel and be the best. While many parents try to communicate this message to their son or daughter, sometimes the child really doesn't hear it.

- **Will my 12-year-old daughter feel socially out of place when she's playing with 13-year-old girls?** Many times parents overlook the social aspects of their child playing on a team with same-age friends and buddies. That's a vital part of sports, and especially important to the enjoyment of the game for the kids. If they don't enjoy that element—or find that they really don't have any friends on the team because of the age difference—then that reality can put a real damper on the child's desire to want to play up and work hard at her sport.

Again, as a parent, you have to use your own common sense and good judgment to determine whether playing up will be a good move for your son or daughter. Yes, it's always wonderful and thrilling to have one's athletic child be considered for moving up. But as a concerned sports parent, try to take the long-range and all-encompassing view to see whether "playing up" is the best thing for your child.

What do you do if you're not sure? The best approach, I have found, is to try to find a combination of both approaches. That is, let your child play on teams within the same age bracket as their peers. Yes, they may dominate, but they will at least enjoy the company of their friends from school. At the same time, see if you can find an older team in your community with whom your child can at least practice some of the time. If you can arrange this, your youngster will have the best of both worlds: they can still enjoy their sport with their friends and buddies, but they can also have the chance to compete against older children without the pressure of having to do extraordinarily well.

Remember, we're talking about kids of middle school age here. There's no rush to push them through the athletic system in such a hurry that it may backfire on them and you.

Specialization in Middle School

It's usually during the middle school years that kids have to start confronting coaches who want them to specialize in just one sport. These days, it's not uncommon for a high school coach to approach a young and talented athlete in middle school and say something like:

"Joey, I know you play a lot of different sports, and that's fine. But let me tell you this . . . if you concentrate on soccer and only soccer, then in my opinion, you've got a real shot at developing into something quite special."

That's a fairly hefty compliment coming from a high school coach to a kid in 7th or 8th grade. Invariably, the youngster is thrilled and his parents share his joy when he tells them what the varsity soccer coach said. But after the original enthusiasm begins to wear off, the young talented athlete then asks his parents: "What does the coach mean about focusing only on soccer? Does he mean I have to stop playing basketball and baseball? I really love soccer, but I love playing those sports too."

It's a difficult choice for anyone to make, but it's especially difficult for a kid who's 13 years old. First off, most kids who are terrific in one sport usually tend to be terrific in a variety of sports. Their natural God-given athleticism translates well from, as in Joey's case, soccer to basketball to baseball. He may be outstanding in soccer, but chances are he's also outstanding in baseball and basketball. Second, lots of kids feel that they don't want to have to make this decision at an early age; they enjoy the change of seasons and sports and don't want to just play one sport 365 days a year.

If your son or daughter is feeling pressured in this way, first understand that it's a wonderful compliment for a high school coach just to deliver such nice praise to your child. That really is something special. But after you have some time to digest it, then sit down with your child and see what they want to do. Maybe they really do want to focus all of their energies into just one sport. If that's the case, then there's no reason why they can't specialize. But on the other hand, if they still want to keep playing a variety of sports, then that's a fine choice as well. Remember: **there's no guaranteed pathway to success in sports.** A great deal of the time you and your child have to go with your instincts, and many times, you go with what is the most fun for your child.

The ultimate question is this: will specializing in a sport definitively give my son or daughter an edge against the kids who don't specialize? Well, in terms of gaining more game experience and more practice time in that sport, absolutely. And that extra game experience and practice will certainly be evident as they enter into the high school junior varsity and varsity ranks. So from that perspective, it will definitely help.

But in the long run, that extra advantage seems to disappear. By the time the kids are juniors or seniors in high school, the disparity between those youngsters who have specialized in one sport versus those who have played a variety of sports begins to become smaller and smaller. Why? Because the elite non-specialized athletes at those ages have honed extra skills in a variety of sports (e.g., sprinting, leaping, passing, anticipating physical contact) that help to level the playing field against those kids who have only played one sport. It's almost as though no matter what pathway your child takes, ultimately all the kids reach a certain finish line; and those who truly have superior athletic ability are the ones who become the stars, no matter what sport or sports they played.

Let's look at a couple of examples to illustrate this fact.

Example #1: New Jersey has long been a hotbed for amateur soccer. Each fall, thousands of kids sign up to play for elite travel teams. And a good number of these kids are quickly told by their travel team coaches to focus exclusively on soccer if they want to progress to the next level beyond high school (i.e. college).

But arguably the best young soccer prospect to come out of New Jersey is the star goalkeeper for the New York/New Jersey Metrostars, Tim Howard. When Tim was a kid growing up, he loved playing soccer; he also loved playing basketball. In fact, he played hoops right through high school where he was a key member of his high school basketball team that won the state championship. In short, he didn't find it necessary to give up basketball in order to play only soccer all year round.

Example #2: Carl Morris made headlines as a talented wide receiver at Harvard in recent years, and is now looking forward to a long career in the NFL. But what's curious about Carl is that when he was growing up, he didn't play any tackle football until he was a junior in high school. And even as a junior, he didn't play very much.

But that's not to say Carl wasn't involved in athletics. In fact he was a most talented basketball player in high school with terrific hands, jumping ability, and coordination. When the Harvard football coach, Tim

Murphy, saw Carl perform in a high school basketball game, he had a hunch that Morris' athletic skills would translate nicely into college football. And indeed, they have. He's now considered one of the top prospects in the NFL. Not too bad for a kid who never specialized in football.

Example #3: How about this as an example of extreme specialization: Nick Browne plays college football and soccer—and does both in the same season!

In the fall of 2001, Nick Browne served as the star placekicker for the Texas Christian University football team. Not only was he a star for his team, he was good enough to be one of the top-ranked Division 1 kickers in the nation. And, during the same time of year, Nick also starred as a midfielder on the TCU soccer team. Now here's the kicker (so to speak): Nick led both the TCU football team and the soccer team in scoring! (*New York Times*, October 18, 2002)

Dealing with Adversity in Adolescence

It's during this time period that many kids will often encounter the first real road bump on their way to a successful sports career. Adversity can come in many different forms to a young athlete: coping with an injury, not making the team, not getting much playing time, dealing with a difficult coach, and so forth. There are all kinds of adversity that can befall a young athlete. **And the truth is, it's the very rare top athlete who doesn't encounter adversity at one point or another in their career.**

As a sports parent, it's during these times of stress and frustration that your youngster will turn to you for guidance and inspiration. To that end, it's critically important that you send the right message to your child so that they can transform the immediate, short-term pain of adversity into a long-term plan for self-improvement.

How is that accomplished? Try this 3-step approach:

1. When your child comes to you filled with anguish and tears over some recent development (e.g., didn't make the team, coach doesn't like them, not enough playing time, etc.), your first reaction is to want to console them. That's fine. But then let them talk out their feelings. Make eye contact. Do not have any distractions. Let your child simply "get it all out of their system."

No, you don't have to offer any constructive criticism during this time. You don't have to go into lecture mode. You don't have to relate how you coped with setbacks in your life. **Don't do any of that!** Just let your child cope with the real pain that they're going through, and simply serve for the moment as a deeply caring parent.

In other words, allow your son or daughter to have a good cry. Bottling up their emotions will only frustrate them even more, so give them the unconditional freedom to express themselves. It's during these parent/child moments that hugs are definitely in order. So give them!

2. Wait until a day or two passes before you ask about the details of their setback. Again, be an active listener and pay careful attention to what they want to say. After they have said their piece, it's now your time to point out that adversity is a part of all sports, and the real question is not how they could encounter such a hurdle, but how they will handle it.

Tell him or her the Michael Jordan story—about how Michael was cut from his high school basketball team when he was a sophomore. But rather than just walk away and tell his friends that the "coach was a jerk" or that he "was the victim of politics," Jordan took a different approach. He pushed his disappointment off to the side, and then found the courage to ask the varsity coach what he needed to work on to make the team next year.

For the next 12 months, Jordan worked on his game, so much so that when he became a junior in high school, he not only made the roster, but he also became a starter. At this point in his career, was Jordan considered the greatest basketball player of all time? No, not even close. He was just happy to have made the starting five. Besides, there were lots of other players in North

Carolina (where Jordan grew up) who were considered to be much better college prospects than Michael.

Keep this in perspective. When Jordan was a high school student, he probably had dreams—as most young athletes do—of perhaps someday playing in college and then the NBA. But if you had asked anyone in Jordan's hometown of Wilmington, NC, whether this was going to happen, you would have been laughed at and gotten the reply: "Michael Jordan make the NBA? Heck, he couldn't even make his high school team!"

Of course, you and the rest of the world know the ending of this story. Jordan kept working at his game, developed his God-given skills, got a little taller, and, by the time he was a senior at the University of North Carolina, he was considered one of the best players in the country.

The moral of the story? Jordan turned a short-term disappointment— not making his high school team—into a long-range success story. In other words, he found the drive and strength within himself to overcome this setback and make his game even stronger. He transformed a negative emotion into a positive drive.

3. Continue to gauge how your child is handling the aftermath of the setback. Hopefully, with your guidance through the first two steps of the process, they will be on their way to learning how to transform a bitter disappointment into a positive force—the best possible outcome for any athlete. It's not easy, especially when a young one is still psychologically feeling down about the setback they have just gone through. That's why, as a sports parent, you have to give the youngster enough time to recover and to want to bounce back from this encounter with adversity. While you can stand by and offer bits of tender encouragement and praise, ultimately the transformation has to come from within the youngster.

But once the transformation comes about, their sense of purpose will practically surprise you. It's almost as though they will have used that bitter pill of adversity as a springboard to truly launch themselves into their sport. They will now use that setback as the mainspring to keep their inner drive going. As a sports parent, when you witness this development, you don't have to say much—except to praise your child for having the courage to fight back. It's a life lesson that will serve them long after their playing days are over.

Will all young athletes bounce back from adversity and develop this kind of self-drive? Unfortunately, no. For some, the pain of disappointment might be too much for them to swallow. They will either turn away from that sport forever, or they will start to focus on another sport they play. Or, in some cases, they will just turn away from sports entirely and decide to focus on another aspect of their life.

If your child has gone through the severe disappointment of not making a team, or of being cut, you should, of course, offer strong and sincere parental sympathy. Along those lines, try to get your child to talk and open up about their frustration. Let them simply get their emotions off their chest. That's important, and it's important that you just listen rather than go into parental lecture mode.

If your child does, in fact, have a strong passion for their sport, then after a few days they will most likely bounce back and will want to go out and play. But during this time when they're hurting, it's essential that you give them some space to let them sort their feelings out. Be compassionate, but give them some room.

The youngsters who do decide to bounce back with a heightened determination are the ones you will find working out on their own in the backyard, working on their jump shot, skating on the frozen pond long after everyone else has gone in, or hitting a tennis ball against a practice wall in the summertime heat. Those are the young athletes who have learned this vitally important lesson of coping with—and overcoming—adversity.

Does this mean that they will go on to become the next Michael Jordan? No, of course there are no guarantees like that. But what they **will** take away from this very disappointing situation is an inner sense of self-confidence and a stronger sense of purpose. Best of all, if they ever encounter another disappointment or setback in their life, they'll be much more equipped for coping with it.

And by the way, there are literally hundreds of stories like that of Michael Jordan. Young athletes who were told they were too small, or too slow, or not good enough—and they all went on to overcome this adversity and become athletic stars. Indeed, it's the rare athlete who hasn't encountered serious adversity in their career. There are lots of stories to choose from, but the one I recall the most is that of Steve Young, the great quarterback for the San Francisco 49ers.

Steve Young, Benchwarmer

When Steve enrolled as a freshman at Brigham Young University, he was stunned to find himself not listed as the number one or number two QB on the roster. In fact, he was listed as number eight on the depth chart! He was considered to be the third string QB on the BYU junior varsity. And although Young had been an outstanding QB at Greenwich High School in Greenwich, CT, even he had to admit that the other seven QBs on the BYU roster threw the football better than he did.

Steve was inconsolable. He wanted to quit. He wanted to go back home to Connecticut and think about whether he should change colleges. But when he finally talked it all over with his father, Steve's Dad convinced him to stay at BYU and to work at his craft. And that's just what Steve did. By the time he was a senior, Steve was clearly one of the top QBs in the country. Now he's an NFL Hall of Famer. Not too bad for an 18-year-old kid who was 8th string!

Again, there are all sorts of stories like Steve Young's. **Adversity should be used to make a young athlete better and stronger—not as a reason to pack it in.**

Preventing Burnout in Middle Schoolers

Ultimately, every youngster will decide for himself or herself when they've reached the point in their athletic career where they are not going to go any further. They may sense that the competition is just becoming too tough, or that they don't have the necessary physical abilities to compete at a higher level, or that they have just reached a saturation level where the sport is no longer a burning passion for them. In any case, all kids will come to that decision point eventually.

But all this being a given, it's also clear that too many kids today are simply "burning out" and quitting sports for none of the above reasons. And they're burning out in huge percentages at the 7th and 8th grade levels. Most psychologists and pediatricians say this is happening (according to most reports, 3 out of 4 kids who play organized sports will quit all sports by the time they're 13) because kids are being pushed too hard into organized sports at too early an age. In effect, because of overzealous sports parents who can't wait to have their little one become a star, kids are playing on competitive teams when they're 5 or 6 years old. And then they begin to spend just about every hour after school and on the weekends either practicing or playing in games or trying out for better teams.

Take a tip from NFL Hall of Famer Kellen Winslow. He didn't start playing organized football until he was a senior in high school in Illinois. But his so-called lack of experience didn't hurt his football career. Kellen ended up at the University of Missouri before going on to a spectacular career with the San Diego Chargers. Even as a player, Winslow noticed that burnout was a real concern. "I remember one guy I played with on the Chargers. He was in his second year with the team, and he had been playing football for 12 years total. I was near the end of my career, and I had only been playing 12 years myself." (*Los Angeles Times*, Nov. 8, 2002)

So when Kellen became a dad himself, it wasn't surprising that he didn't encourage his son, Kellen Jr., to play football until he was in high school. Bear in mind that Kellen Jr. is now one of the nation's top tight ends himself at the University of Miami, and he stands 6'5", 235 lbs. Why didn't the dad let his own son play tackle football? Because Kellen Sr. didn't want his son—who could have easily played youth football from age 8—to run the risk of burning out from the sport.

Kellen Winslow may have very good instincts when it comes to preventing burnout. Studies show that by the time youngsters are in 7th or 8th grade (ages 12–13), kids will often show the first signs of tedium or frustration with all of their sports training. What's more, as they begin to develop their own individual voice as a pre-teenager, they'll note that their school-age peers are now becoming much more involved than ever before with social events, such as dances, sleepover parties, birthday parties, celebrations, and all the other usual social goings-on for teenagers.

Not surprisingly, all kids—even athletic ones—want to be part of this social scene. This is a normal part of the teenage maturation process. But it's very difficult to balance a young athlete's demanding sports schedule with a crammed social calendar. To me, this is all part of the problem when it comes to potential burnout in kids. Children, for the first time in their lives, may have to choose between going to a party or going to a practice.

For many children at this age, they begin to look upon practice (or even a game) as being more of an obligation or a task rather than a joyful occasion. Sadly, once this transformation begins—**when play turns into work**—then it's not too long after that burnout can occur. Take a look at this typical sports parent/young athlete conversation:

"Mom, Sarah is having a sleepover party Friday night with all of my friends . . . can I go?"

"Well, unfortunately, kids your age rarely get any sleep at those kinds of parties, and you have a travel-team soccer tryout the next morning. You want to be fresh and ready for that. You know what, honey—I don't think it's a good idea for you to go to the party."

"But Mom, everybody else is going! Why do I always have to be left out?"

You can just see the kinds of conflicts that are going to occur with the daughter who wants to be with her friends, and her mother who wants her to get a good night's rest before soccer practice. And of course, the same kinds of conflicts occur with boys this age as well. If this kind of scheduling conflict continues throughout the year, more often than not, the child will decide to quit travel soccer rather than give up her social scene and time with friends. Even worse, once a child walks away from a sport, they rarely ever come back to it. They'll rationalize this decision by simply saying something like:

"I really wasn't having that much fun with travel soccer anyway" or *"I didn't have many friends on the team"* or *"The coach was too demanding"* or some other excuse that allows the child to walk away from this competitive situation without a fight. For the parents, this decision to simply throw away years of athletic training can seem incomprehensible. But for the pre-teenager, this life choice seems obvious and normal to them.

What's the solution? First off, the truth is that kids this young shouldn't be forced to make these kinds of impossible decisions. Sports should still be about having fun. To that end, it would be nice if travel team coaches were smart enough to recognize that middle schoolers do have very busy social schedules. Since this is the time in life when many kids do burn out, it would make all the sense in the world for coaches to give the individual kids some leeway when it comes to making all the practices and games.

As a parent, you have to be very careful to walk a delicate line between your child's desires to be with their friends and their commitment to the team. The best solution is to find a travel team in which the coach is sensitive to the fact that kids in middle school do not want to miss parties, celebrations, sleepovers, etc. The smart coach can address these concerns with the parents before the year begins, and ideally come to some sort of compromise. For example, the coach may say that it's okay for the child to miss two or three Saturday morning practices so long as the coach knows about it several weeks ahead of time. Or that a player can miss the occasional game because of a social conflict.

Does this mean I advocate that middle schoolers should not take their team commitments seriously? Of course not. In fact, I'm saying just the opposite. And in order to help kids become even more committed to the team and the rigorous practice/game schedule they will face, it's wise to give them a chance to have some breathing room to just be a kid. It's my belief and experience that those middle schoolers who feel that they can enjoy the best of both worlds (i.e. socializing and athletics) are less likely to burn out from their sports involvement.

As a sports parent who wants the best for their young athlete, be aware of these burnout concerns. They are real, and again, the best way to avoid them is by meeting first with the coach and other parents well before the season begins to discuss giving the kids a break here and there.

Motivation and the Middle Schooler

The flip side of preventing burnout is trying to make certain that your child continues to be strongly motivated to do well in sports. Yes, of course, a steady diet of praise from you and his or her coach is essential, but deep down, the real drive to do well must come from the young athlete.

It may sound like a cliché, but it really is true that you can teach a kid all the Xs and Os of any sport and encourage them to play their best, but you can't teach them to have an inner, burning passion for their sport or sports. This is the bottom line when it comes to providing real motivation. As the old coaches say, "Either they have it . . . or they don't."

That harsh reality is often frustrating for Moms and Dads who see that their child has a tremendous gift of athletic ability, but doesn't seem to have that burning desire to push him or herself to a higher level. Many parents have come to me with the following complaint:

"I'll come home from work on a beautiful spring day, and there's my 7th grader, sitting in front of the TV or playing a video game for hours. When

I suggest that he go outside to take advantage of the great weather and play a little ball, he'll just blow me off.

"I'll think to myself, 'My gosh! How can I get this kid to go outside and work on his game?' Sure, he's doing very well for his age bracket in our town, but there are thousands of other kids across the country who are his age and have similar athletic talent, but they're out practicing instead of watching TV."

You can hear the exasperation in these parents' voices. And while I'm certainly sympathetic to their frustration, I also come back to the reality that **the desire has to come from inside the kid—not from outside pushing by the parent.**

Does that mean that the parent shouldn't say anything to their son or daughter? No, in fact, I do encourage parents to have a little straightforward session with their child, and to say something like:

Parent: "I just want you to know that it's clear to me and certainly clear to you that you have been given some extraordinary athletic gifts from God. There are lots and lots of kids who play sports who wish that they could do some of the neat things that you do during a game.

"But that being said, just having great talent is not enough if you want to continue to succeed. When you were in elementary school, your talent was all you needed. But now that you're in middle school and getting ready for high school, you're going to have to understand that your talent will only carry you so far. It's that inner drive that most great athletes have that will push you to greater success.

"But that inner drive is something that I can't teach you or give to you. It's something you have to feel inside yourself—that you want to go out, work on your game, and make it a real passion for yourself. Because talent plus determination makes for real champions."

And that's the end of your little speech. Don't worry—you'll know within a few days whether it had any real impact on your son or daughter.

Insider's Trick: Motivation via a Third Party

Sometimes, the relationship between parent and child is such that the child really doesn't want to hear from Mom or Dad. And they certainly won't sit for a lecture about why they should develop an inner drive in sports. Says the 12-year-old: *"What the heck is wrong with Dad? Why is he on my back to go out and practice basketball more? Doesn't he see that I'm already the leading scorer on my team?"*

This reaction is all too common, and parents will often feel that they have stepped over the line from being the kid's biggest booster to having become a pushy sports parent. In order to avoid this kind of situation, many times it might be appropriate to ask a third party to come in and have a brief chat with the youngster.

Selecting that third party has to be well thought out. The ideal choice would be an adult who is either a top coach, or a top player, or an individual in your community who is highly respected for his or her advice and opinions. You should seek out that individual, ask for their help, and see if they would be kind enough to intervene and talk with your child about their game and desire.

Of course, this should all be planned and mapped out without the child's knowledge. Otherwise, he or she will very likely see through the entire interaction as a sham. But if you can find that adult who has no real connection to your son or daughter, and if that individual will talk to your kid in a positive way, then there's a much greater chance of your child listening attentively to what that person has to say.

For example, let's say your child is a talented baseball player. For a 12-year-old, he dominates his same-age peers in the local youth league. But you, as a parent, know that your son rarely takes any extra batting practice, never works on his pitching, and doesn't do much running. He prefers to spend his afternoons just hanging out. He feels he has the luxury of not working hard because everything in baseball has come so easy to him.

You also know he won't pay attention to you if you talk to him about practicing more. But if you found a well-respected high school or college coach in your area, or even a professional ballplayer, to come over and talk with your son, your athlete might get a whole different perspective. Here are a couple of sample scripts that a third-party adult might employ with a 12-year-old:

Third Party Script #1: "You know, Mike, when I was your age, everything came real easy to me in sports. I was always the best, so I never practiced. Didn't have to. But as I got older and got into high school, I found that the rest of the kids were now beginning to catch up to me in terms of ability.

"But I was lucky. One day, one of my coaches came over to me and said that I had better start working hard, or all these other kids on the team were going to bypass me. He even told me that some of the other kids had caught up to me, and in some cases had already passed me! I was stunned to hear that! But after I got through that shock, that served as my wake-up call, and from that day, I started to work, and work hard."

Third Party Script #2: "Mike, I've been watching you over the last few weeks, and you know what? You have some great ability. That's the good news. You really could develop into something special. But here's the bad news. Unless you put some real effort into your practices, you're not going to get much better than you are right now. That's right, you will have peaked as a 12-year-old. Too bad, too, because all you have to do is develop a real work ethic, and you could be something really special in the years to come."

No matter what kind of approach or script you use, you're trying to get your child to pay attention and understand that his or her innate talent is not going to be enough in the long run. Simply telling your youngster this yourself may not register with them. That's precisely why using a well-respected third party adult is often the best way to go when it comes to motivating your child. It may not always work, but this is guaranteed: it will give your child something to really think about, and to think about in a positive way. As a sports parent, that's exactly what you're trying to accomplish.

Try it with your middle school youngster. More often than not, the young athlete will respond in a most positive way.

CHAPTER FOUR:
Travel Teams—What Every
Sports Parent Should Know

Up until around the mid-1980s, the concept of a "travel team" for a youth sport program just didn't exist in the form that we know today. Yes, there was the occasional All-Star team that would challenge an All-Star team from a neighboring town to an occasional game or two. And there were some regional or citywide leagues in which teams would "travel" to other fields and gyms to play their opponents. But the idea of having a set team of select players who practiced together and who played in a competitive league against other travel teams from far and wide had yet to be realized.

Some sports sociologists have suggested that travel teams were first introduced into the United States in the 1980s by fervent adult soccer players who were eager to have their own kids play highly competitive soccer as well. These fanatic soccer parents were frustrated that the traditional soccer season in America was limited to a few months in the fall. Indeed, they wanted their kids to play soccer all year round, and so they started their own "travel" soccer clubs that competed against other "travel" soccer clubs during the fall, winter, and spring seasons.

After witnessing the success of these soccer travel teams—and seeing how the young soccer players accelerated their soccer talent—the parents of kids who played other sports, like basketball, baseball, and ice hockey, decided that they wanted their kids to enjoy a lengthened playing season as well. Before too long, travel teams were introduced in all of these sports, and the concept has grown rapidly everywhere across the nation.

These days, it's the rare town or community that doesn't have at least one travel team per age bracket and in a variety of sports (soccer, basketball, hockey, baseball, etc.). Some travel programs start as early as age 7 (which to me is quite extreme), and travel teams exist right through the high school years. To me, travel teams at the high school age are the most important to play on, because travel teams are routinely scouted by college coaches. Bear in mind, though, that no matter what age level your child decides to begin playing for a travel team, he or she will inevitably have to go through one or several tryout sessions to make the team. And these try-outs can be extremely daunting, mainly because there are usually many kids trying out for only a few available spots on the travel team roster.

What Is a Travel Team?

Travel teams go by different names. Sometimes they are called select teams, or premier teams, or just All-Star teams. But no matter what their label is, travel teams generally are regarded as being comprised of the so-called best athletes in a particular age bracket in a given sport. Unlike the local recreational "rec" programs where anybody (regardless of athletic ability) who registers will be placed on a team and will typically get to play a lot in each game, travel teams make it clear that they're trying to attract only the better, more athletically inclined youngsters.

On a rec team, which is usually organized and run by the local recreational department in town, the emphasis is almost always on getting all the kids into the games, rather than worry about the final score of the game. Nobody tends to worry too much about making all the games or practices; the kids on each team simply show up to play on the team when their schedule permits. Parents may show up occasionally to watch a game, but for the most part, the local rec department staffers take care of all the coaching and organizing. The parents don't often get involved in coaching a team. The rec department normally places more emphasis on instruction and, quite honestly, on making sure the kids just have a good time.

But with a travel team, the priorities are shifted substantially. Here, the coaches want the kids to make a major commitment to the team. Often that means a six-month commitment, where routinely every weekend consists of games and practices, sometimes several hours away from home. There are usually one or two practices during the week as well. Three-day weekends during the year, such as Labor Day or Columbus Day or Memorial Day and the like, are often filled with tournaments that can last all three days.

If all this sounds like a major commitment not only by your young athlete, but also by you, well, you're right. Since kids can't drive themselves to practices or games, you have to be available to chauffeur them to all their travel team commitments. This can become quite vexing if both you and your spouse work during the day, and your work schedule conflicts with your child's travel team schedule. And if you have more than one child who plays sports, well, then all the chauffeuring to and from practices can become quite a challenge. And don't expect to have too much sympathy from the travel team coach about missed practices or games; for the most part, they don't want to hear about your concerns in getting your kid to a game or practice. They just want the kid to be there, on time, and with no exceptions or excuses.

I know this experience firsthand. When our son John was 12, he played for a travel hockey program based in Suffern, New York. He was thrilled when he made the travel "B" team. But what I didn't realize at the time was that the team played in a New Jersey-based hockey league. That meant that from early September through the end of February, every Saturday and Sunday featured games all over the state of New Jersey. I can't even try to estimate how many thousands of miles I drove up and down the New Jersey Turnpike during that fall and winter with my son, going to his hockey games throughout New Jersey. Even worse, practice sessions at the rink were usually at 6 a.m.; that called for some very, very early mornings, especially because we lived about 45 miles from the rink.

Looking back, I really wonder whether the experience was worth it. That is, I'm sure my son benefited from playing against good hockey competition, but was that fair to the rest of my family? Was it even fair to my son, who had to get used to doing homework in the car and not being able to attend his friends' weekend parties and get-togethers? Was it fair to my wife and our two daughters, who rarely saw me or their brother on the weekends? I don't have the answers to those questions, but as a travel team parent, you have to be aware of these sacrifices.

Who Picks the Travel Team?

As you might imagine, trying to determine who are the "best athletes" for a particular age bracket in a particular sport is open to plenty of debate and discussion—some of it quite animated and heated. Most travel teams have tryouts for their potential team members. Usually, these tryouts are organized and conducted by the coach, or coaches, who will run the team.

Tryouts vary according to the travel team: some may last just one practice session, while others may go through a few weekends. Because the travel team is run by the travel team coach (and bear in mind that quite literally **anyone** can announce to the community that he or she is going to set up and coach a travel team), it's the coach who determines how many tryout sessions there will be, when they will be, and who will do the evaluations.

Bear in mind that, in some cases, the travel team coach will have already invited certain kids to be on the team, so that they either don't have to show up for the tryout, or if they do go, they know they can relax

because they've already been selected to be on the team. Obviously, if
your child is one of those "chosen" kids, you have no problem. But if your
child was not one of the pre-invited kids, then a tryout session can be very
stressful for them and for you.

Let's return to the issue of talent evaluation. As a sports parent, you
have to be more than a bit cautious about who's doing the grading of the
kids trying out. Especially if there's a tryout fee involved, you have
every right to ask the travel coach ahead of time how the tryouts are
going to be conducted, and who's going to be doing the judging. If you're
brave enough, you can even ask if there are certain kids who have
already been selected. Just one word of advice: be certain to approach
the travel coach with a gentle smile on your face. Do not present yourself in any way as being confrontational or else you might make the
coach defensive; if you do, that will send him or her the wrong message
about you and your child.

Of course, in those communities where lots of kids try out for a particular travel team, there can be considerable anxiety about whether the
evaluations are rigged and that the team is already pre-selected. This is
especially true when just one coach is making all the selections. I can
recall when my hockey-playing son was trying out for a travel team in
Darien, Connecticut. As I recall, there were 17 slots on the team, but
close to 75 kids were trying out. The Darien Youth Hockey board got
together and, rather than allow the travel team head coach to complete the
evaluations of all the players by himself, decided to hire a group of
hockey coaches from the state of Rhode Island to come in for a couple of
weekends and analyze the 75 skaters.

Why did the Darien board do this? Simply because they didn't want to
be accused of favoritism or nepotism when it came to selecting the 17
kids for the travel team. By bringing in several coaches from out of state,
the Darien board was able to make the parents feel secure that at least the
tryouts would be handled fair and square. At each tryout, each youngster
was given a sheet of paper with a big black number on it. Each child had

to pin that number to the back of his jersey. Kids who happened to wear jerseys with their names already on it were asked to take those off, and put on a jersey with no name.

When the final list was posted, sadly, there were lots of disappointed kids and parents, but at least they walked away knowing that the tryouts were conducted fairly. Ironically, some of the kids who had been on that travel team the year before didn't make the cut the second year. They were, of course, furious, and some even protested to the Darien board. But the board pointed out that it made no difference where the kids had played last year. All that mattered was how they performed during the several weekends of evaluations this year, and that the evaluations were done by an independent group of coaches.

To my mind, this is perhaps the finest kind of travel team evaluation— where the team coaches are not involved and evaluators from outside the community are brought in to make judgments on the kids. There are, of course, no perfect ways to select a travel team, but this system seems like it's certainly headed in the right direction.

Aren't Travel Coaches Honest?

Yes, of course they are, for the most part. But bear in mind that travel teams are not regulated in any way by local rec departments, or for that matter, by an independent board of directors. Yes, to play in a travel league, there are certain basic rules about a child's age eligibility, and perhaps even residency requirements. But beyond that, as far as coaches go, there are rarely any rules or stipulations regarding a coach's ability to coach, or any concern about his credentials for that matter, including whether the coach has a criminal record of any kind.

As a result, the administration of travel teams is pretty much a case of "Hey, it's my team—and I'm the coach." With that kind of mentality, travel team coaches can usually run tryouts as they see fit, decide who plays where in the games, decide which kids play the most, and decide which kids rarely play at all. Naturally, if your kid is seen by the coach as being one of the star players, none of these issues is going to concern you very much. But for every star athlete on the team, there are numerous others who find themselves mystified, confused, and frustrated to find themselves playing a position they don't really want to play, or even worse, to find themselves spending most of their time on the bench watching the other kids play.

An important note: Let me make one major point regarding travel teams before I delve deeper into this chapter. While there are certainly lots of potential pitfalls that can accompany a travel team experience, at least theoretically, **there's no reason why your son or daughter's experience on a travel team can't be a joyful, fun-filled, and quite productive experience.** But all that being said, it's the smart parent who takes the time to do one's homework before allowing one's child to sign up for a travel team tryout.

Six Points to Consider When Evaluating Travel Teams

1. Consider getting more information. For starters, if you feel that your kid is ready and eager to try out for a travel team, take the time to ask questions of other parents in your community whose own kids have played for that travel team in previous years. Most of the time these parents will not only be glad to answer your questions, but they'll often provide details about matters you may not think to ask about. Listen carefully to these parents' comments, and take notes, as they can give you invaluable firsthand information about the time commitment, the financial expense, the head coach, the assistant coaches, the other parents, the competition, and so on.

And remember, the more parents you contact and the more opinions you can find, the better informed you'll be about whether this is the right step for your child. Sometimes, especially if the youngster is athletically talented but has not gone through a growth spurt yet, playing on a travel team where they are going to be one of the smaller athletes will not be good for their sense of self-confidence or self-esteem. If this is the case with your youngster, there's nothing wrong with letting another year go by (and letting them grow some more) before they try out for a travel squad.

Why this advice? Because it's been my observation over the years that **most travel team coaches prefer to play the youngsters who are physically larger than their peers.** It makes no difference what the sport is, or how much athletic skill the larger child may have in relation to the smaller athlete. The bottom line is that travel team coaches like to have bigger kids on their team, and the bigger kids usually end up getting the most playing time in the games.

There's an old saying in sports: *"The big kids have to show that they can't—and the little kids have to show that they can."* This belief, in my opinion, started with travel teams.

2. Consider how much playing time your child can expect. Ask parents with firsthand experience how many kids are on the team, and how much playing time each kid gets. For example, if it's a travel soccer team, and the coach carries a roster of 20 girls (only 11 play at one time), it's clear that a lot of the girls are going to be spending a good chunk of each game on the bench. Remember—with most travel teams, the coach expects a firm and solid commitment that your child will go to every game. And so most of those 20 girls will always show up, and will expect to play—and play a lot—in each game. With a roster of 20 kids, it's clear that there's only going to be limited playing time for all the kids on the team.

By the way, you've probably already recognized that the number-one issue for most parents of travel team players is their child's playing time in the games. Unlike a rec program where kids are guaranteed to play in at least half of the game, travel team coaches are under no such obliga-tion. It's entirely up to the coach to decide who starts, who plays a lot, and who sits on the bench. If your child is one of those kids who end up on the bench most of the time, you have to wonder whether he or she would be better served—and would have more fun—playing for perhaps another team where they'd play, and play a lot, in the games. **Remember this basic truth: your child will not get any better sitting on the bench and watching other kids play.**

Also remember that you have every right to ask the coach about your child's playing time. Especially if you're paying for your athlete to be on the team, you can certainly ask the coach if you can chat with him or her about your child's progress (or lack thereof). Naturally, you never want to confront the coach on game day (either before, during, or after the game). But certainly you can contact the coach during the week, or perhaps talk to him or her after a practice.

During that conversation, you should never be confrontational or demanding in your demeanor. Rather, you can start the discussion with an approach like this:

"Coach, I wanted to talk to you for a moment or two about Michelle . . . as you know, she doesn't seem to be logging as much playing time in the games as the other kids on the team, and I was wondering if you can help us get to a point where Michelle can get more playing time. . . ."

An approach like this is both civil and considerate, but to the point. And once you ask your question, listen carefully to what the coach says. She might say:

"You know, Mr. Smith, you're right, I haven't been fair to your daugh-ter. She really has been getting shortchanged in the games, and I'll be cer-tain to make sure she gets her equal share of playing time in the future."

But unfortunately, chances are that the coach won't say that. She'll most likely say something like:

"Your daughter is a wonderful and bright girl, Mr. Smith, but she really needs to work on her footwork and speed. . . ." Or:

"Your daughter is just a tad too small physically compared to the other kids at this age, and I don't want to place her in a key situation where she might get hurt. . . ." Or even:

"Honestly, Mr. Smith, this is a travel team, and my mandate right from the beginning is to win all the games. And to do that, I have to play the best players. Your daughter is still developing, but she's not one of the stronger players yet. Look, I'll get your daughter into the games whenever I can, but I can't make any promises. . . ."

When you hear comments like these (especially the latter), rather than try and debate the coach about the merits of his comments, you might want to take a step back and wonder whether this is the best approach for your child in sports. It's pretty clear that the coach is not going to change his opinion of your youngster in terms of more playing time, and you have to wonder what kind of negative impact all this bench-warming is going to have on your daughter's self-confidence.

Remember—this is a travel team. Your son or daughter was chosen for this team because of their superior athletic skills. That's important. But now they're getting limited playing time. Wouldn't it make more sense for them to go back and play on perhaps a slightly less strong team where they could get lots more playing time? In addition to further developing their skills, it would be good for their self-confidence to be a "star" player again. Besides, it's always a lot more fun to actually *play* in the games.

3. Consider the coach's demeanor. Do some scouting of your own to determine the coach's sideline behavior during the games. Is he a yeller and screamer? Does he vent his wrath on individual kids if they make a mistake? Does he offer lots of praise, or is he just critical? How does the coach interact with the referees or umpires? Is he out of control with the officials, or does he exhibit good sportsmanship at all times?

Most top college and high school coaches follow the "5-to-1" ratio when it comes to motivating kids today. **That means 5 parts praise to 1 part criticism.** Kids today—especially young athletes on travel teams— need lots and lots of praise from the coach if they are going to perform well. Critical comments should be minimal, and should be couched in very non-threatening terms.

Unfortunately, too many travel team coaches see themselves as disciples of the legendary pro football coach Vince Lombardi. The myths about Lombardi portray him as a hard-driving, no-nonsense disciplinarian. Too many travel team coaches feel that's the best way to approach kids: be loud, be demanding, and don't be afraid to single a kid out during a game for making a mistake.

This is, as you might imagine, the absolute worst way to work with kids today. Kids don't want to be criticized, they don't want to be yelled at, and they don't want to be humiliated in front of their parents and teammates during a game. If the coach of your child's travel team has the reputation for being this way, again, you had better think twice as to whether your child is ready for this kind of "tough-guy" approach. The truth is, most kids aren't.

By the way, don't be fooled by the coach who openly tells the kids on the team that "Sometimes, I get a little carried away during the games. I might yell some words that I probably shouldn't, or I might say some things that I shouldn't. But don't let those outbursts bother you. It's just that I want so much for the team to do well."

If you hear a travel coach say something like this, ask yourself if you want your child to be exposed to a grown-up who seemingly can't control his or her language or actions during a kids' game. When was the last time you saw New York Yankees manager Joe Torre or California Angels manager Mike Scioscia get visibly upset during a game? They don't; they deal with their frustrations and challenges with quiet resolve. And that's the kind of coach I'd want my child to play for—not an individual who can't control their temper.

4. Consider the coach's commitment. Ask about the coach's frequency of attendance at the practice sessions. There are plenty of travel team coaches who oversee several travel teams at the same time, often overseeing teams from different age brackets. As a result, while they will always be present at the games on the weekends, they may miss a number of weekday practices because of their own scheduling conflicts.

For practice sessions, you may learn that an assistant coach (usually one of the players' father) will be assigned to run the drills. In other words, while the travel head coach insists that your child go to every game and practice, the truth is that he misses lots of practices himself. Besides, you may know very little about the assistant coach and their ability to coach your kid. Commitment should be a two-way street. If you are going to get your kid to all the games and practices, then shouldn't the coach be there as well?

5. Consider the schedule of activities. You also want to know up front about the schedule of games and tournaments planned for the upcoming year. Be wary of the travel team coach who doesn't have a firm schedule yet. He may say that the team can expect to go to several tournaments during the year, but certainly you want to know where they are and when they are so that you can adjust your own family's calendar. The best travel team coaches will not only have their entire game and practice schedule already mapped out and ready to give to you, but they'll have the tournament schedule as well.

6. Consider the issue of total commitment. Some travel coaches are so insistent that their travel team is the top priority for their team members that they demand the kids and their parents sign a contract that commits them to the team. This is probably a bit too much. During the course of the year, there are always going to be conflicts with the schedule. Kids want to go to birthday parties, they want to go on family vacations, and they want to do the kinds of social activities that other kids their age do. Commitment—meaning that a youngster never misses a practice or game except for family emergencies—is an issue that you must address with the coach before signing on for the team. If he refuses to modify his policy, you might want to reconsider whether this is the way you want your child to spend the next six months of his or her life.

The Positive Aspects of Travel Teams

Now that we've run down all the concerns you should have regarding travel teams, let me finish this chapter by mentioning the positive aspects of travel teams.

First, for those kids who really truly love that one sport, and would play it 24/7 if you gave them the chance, playing for a travel team can be a wonderful experience. It allows them to develop their skills in an accelerated fashion—especially if they are fortunate enough to play for a coach who is a good instructor and motivator. That, of course, becomes a win-win situation for your child and their coach.

Playing on a team that demands a tremendous amount of time helps kids learn how to balance their time away from school. Believe it or not, time management skills are very important for young athletes, and learning this basic skill when one is relatively young is actually a real positive take-away for any child.

As one gets a little older, the experience of playing on a travel team also exposes them to more and more possibilities in their sport. It's the travel teams where high school, prep school, and college coaches usually find prospects to watch in the years to come. So, if your child continues to play travel right through middle school and high school, they'll get the kind of exposure that you want for your child.

Finally, travel team coaches are becoming more sensitive to the needs of their players. As the competition heats up, these coaches are realizing that in order to keep all of their kids motivated, they have to work hard to juggle the roster so that all the kids get a chance to play a lot in each game. That's good. And in fact, that's the way it should be.

HEY KIDS! WANT TO JUMP
HIGHER AND RUN FASTER?
TRY PLYOMETRICS

Back in the early 1990s, I worked for the Cleveland Indians as their roving sports psychology coach. I normally spent several weeks each year with the ballplayers, both in the major and the minor leagues. Part of my assignment was to spend time in spring training with the players.

And as a former pro player myself, I had attended many spring training sessions before. And usually in spring training, the daily routine each morning is pretty standard fare. That is, at the designated hour, all the players run a lap or two, and then they break into ranks to do their stretching, sit ups, push ups, and so forth. After about 15 minutes of this preliminary loosening up, the coaches and players break out the bats and balls and go to work on their hitting, fielding, etc.

On one particular spring training day, I was observing the players going through their paces. Yet I was surprised when, at the end of their warm-up session, rather than start throwing the ball around or playing pepper they dutifully lined up on a side field that was covered with all sorts of cones, jump ropes, lines, medicine balls, and other kinds of sporting/fitness paraphernalia. As you might imagine, it was clear that these ballplayers were not going through the typical baseball practice that I was accustomed to.

Curious, I saw the players line up in rows of three, then work on short but quick sprints, or jump over small boxes, or run around cones. I had never seen anything like it! It was as though they were all participating in a series of very basic physical education exercises—exercises that were borrowed from their elementary school days. Upon investigation, I discovered that the players had just been introduced that spring to a new science of conditioning called **plyometrics**.

Don't be surprised if you have never heard this term before. The truth is, most parents haven't. For that matter, very few coaches seem to know of this science either. In short, plyometric exercises are specifically designed to increase an athlete's quickness, speed, agility, and jumping ability. How successful are these exercises? Well, in these days of the early 21st century, **it's now the rare professional or college team that doesn't use some form of plyometrics in its training.** But as mentioned, it seems that very few high school or middle school programs seem to know about plyometrics. That's particularly vexing, because it's those younger athletes who could benefit most from these simple but extremely effective exercises.

As a sports parent, I urge you to find out more about plyometric training and then see if you or a trainer can design a program that suits your child's individual needs (such as speed training, or jumping ability). In my experience, the best source on the subject is a book called *Jumping into Plyometrics* by Dr. Donald A. Chu. In addition, for those athletes who want to focus on increasing their footspeed, visit the web site of Dr. Bob Clark (www.speedscience.com). Dr. Clark, who is a Stanford-trained physician, has studied precisely how the human leg and foot work, and has designed a comprehensive program that, if one pursues it diligently, will most likely enhance their times in a variety of sprints.

Is this science fiction? Well, I've seen plyometrics work myself, and in terms of speed training, Dr. Clark gets big-time results. Athletes from all over the country seek out his counsel on how to improve their foot speed. How does it work? In short, Dr. Clark urges kids to learn how to run on the balls on their feet. Most kids simply run ahead, with their heel landing first before they push off with their toes.

As Dr. Clark points out, we spend a lot of time teaching our kids how to shoot a basketball or how to serve a tennis ball, but we rarely teach them how to run well. And running plays a major factor in most sports. Dr. Clark's plyometric speed training starts first by examining how your child runs, and then builds a program from there.

So What Is a Plyometric Exercise?

First off, the best part about plyometric training is that it doesn't take more than 15–20 minutes a day. Plus it's relatively easy, certainly inexpensive, and mostly painless. It's worth your while to find a certified trainer in your town who is knowledgeable about plyometrics. Then, with their cooperation, have them design a program for your child to follow.

Here are some typical plyometric exercises, as recommended by Greg Brittenham, an assistant coach for the NBA's New York Knicks:

Jump Rope: Every athlete knows how to jump rope. The key here is that when you jump, make certain you stay on your toes, or on the balls of your feet. If you jump rope for, say, 7–10 minutes at a stretch—and stay on your toes while doing it—you'll begin to build up your foot quickness.

Box Run: Find a small wooden box that's no more than 10 inches high. Start with your right foot on top of the box, and with your other foot on the floor. Then, while jumping quickly, simultaneously switch your feet's position so that the left foot is now on the box, and the right one is on the floor. Try doing 10–20 switches, then rest for a minute or two.

Repeat this drill 3–5 times. This is excellent training to increase sprint speed and jumping ability.

Box Jump: Stand with both feet on the same box. Make sure your toes are on the edge of the box, but with your heels hanging over the other edge. Try to jump off the box with both feet, and then jump back on the box as quickly as possible. Concentrate on how quickly you can jump back and forth, from the box to the ground and back again. Jump 10–15 times from floor to box and back again. Then rest for a minute or two. Then do your jumping again. Do this drill 3–5 times. This is excellent training for your vertical leaping ability.

Towel Hop: Spread a towel on the floor. Start at one corner of the towel and do a double leg jump around the towel's edges. Make sure that when you jump, you jump from one corner of the towel to the next. Try doing 3–8 "round trips" around the towel (a round trip is touching all four corners of the towel) at a time. Do the drill 3–5 times, and you'll find that it helps your agility.

Again, these are only a small sampling of the kinds of plyometric exercises that your youngster can do on their own. You can start with kids as young as 8 or 9, and they can stay with them well into their late teens or even older. Remember—more and more professional athletes are doing these exercises than ever before, so if you want your child to get a jump on their competitors, try plyometrics.

Should Young Athletes Weight Train?

When young athletes become entrenched in the world of travel-team sports, they instinctively feel the need to get an edge on their competition wherever they can. Beyond basic calisthenics and plyometrics, there is the weight room.

Merely a generation or two ago, not only were young athletes told not to lift weights, they were in fact told that weight training could be extremely harmful to their athletic ability.

Even today, there are lots of parents (myself included) who were told when they were kids in the 1960s and 70s that one should always avoid the weight room unless one planned on a career as a lineman in football or as an Olympic weightlifter.

These days every serious athlete spends copious amounts of time in weight training. But in the past, athletes in virtually every sport were discouraged from training with weights. Young baseball pitchers were told that lifting weights could make one too muscle-bound, that such a regimen could tighten their biceps too much, and that they could ultimately hurt their pitching arm. Basketball players were told that if they lifted weights to gain more bulk, then they might lose their athleticism and their scoring touch. And the idea that any female athlete might try to do some weight training to tone her muscles was considered laughable. As a result, weight rooms went mostly unused, because except for the occasional football player or wrestler, everybody thought that using weights would be harmful for their athletic career.

Even worse, for those few who did work out with weights, they often had very little guidance in terms of how to train properly. Often you had kids who either lifted too much, or didn't have the right techniques, or just didn't know how to enhance the various parts of their body with weights.

But as with most things in sports, times have changed. These days, kids as young as 11 and 12 are being told that they can start a weight training program, so long as it's strictly supervised by a certified trainer.

So Where Does One Start?

It makes no difference what sport you play. Regardless of whether it's tennis, or football, or lacrosse, or swimming, it's now universally agreed that every young athlete can benefit from weight training. **The key, however, is in making certain that you set up the right kind of training program. And no one training program fits all.** After all, the program for a wrestler most likely will be much different than a program for, say, a soccer player.

As a sports parent, it's up to you to find the right kind of program for your youngster. Here are the steps you have to take:

1. Start with your pediatrician or family physician. This is essential. Let them know that you're thinking about having your son or daughter get involved in a weight training program. Ask your doctor if this makes sense to them. Most of the time, there's no problem. But the physician should know that your child is going to be actively lifting weights, most likely three times a week. If there are any issues about your child's health, your pediatrician will let you know.

Why is checking with the doctor the first step? Because you would much rather know your doctor's concerns (if any) before your child starts, rather than have to get medical treatment after they have been lifting for a period of time.

2. Seek out a local weight training center and/or a particular certified trainer. Start by asking your pediatrician or family doctor if they can make such recommendations. If they cannot do so, ask if they can recommend any local physical therapists. Almost always, physical therapists (who of course do a lot of rehab work for athletes) will have a handy list of reputable weight trainers in your area.

If all that fails, you might place a call to the high school athletic director. Again, you're looking for sources of information here. It's the rare high school athletic director these days who isn't familiar with local weight trainers and the programs they offer.

3. Whatever you do, do not rely upon the advice of other parents or other older athletes. At least not those who simply say, "Sure, I'll be glad to teach your kid about lifting." Weight training, especially for young athletes, has to be monitored carefully and cautiously by someone who specializes in the field.

4. It's vitally important that the trainer ask the right questions regarding your athlete. For example: Why do you want to start weight training? What sport or sports do you play? What part of your body do you want to concentrate on (e.g., legs, upper body, etc.)? How often can you get to the gym? These are the kinds of basic questions that should be asked before your youngster starts to get involved with weight training.

5. How much does the program cost? That's another basic question you should ask the trainer up front. Most weight training programs will last several weeks, and usually will call for lifting at least three times a week. Get the answers to this all up front. Be prepared to spend a few hundred dollars.

6. How soon before my kid starts to see results? The truth is, most kids—especially skinny teenagers—can't wait to see their bodies blossom to reveal rippling muscles. While they should understand that they may not look like Mr. Universe after only two or three weeks of weight training, they will certainly expect to see some sort of physical improvement after a month or so. You can only imagine their frustration when they pose in front of a mirror and don't see much obvious change.

This is when most kids will quit their program. They're working hard, but don't see any tangible results. As their parent, explain to them that the rippling muscles will eventually appear, but that it will take time. How much time depends on the individual athlete, their age, and their genetic make-up.

As a sports parent, you can help your child stick to their weight training program by encouraging them to focus on the actual weight training program and how much progress they're making there. In other words, let's say when they first started doing weight training, the most they could handle on the bench press was three sets (with 10 repetitions each set) of 120 lbs. But now, a month into the program, they can now handle 150 lbs. on the bench press, and are eager to lift more.

That's the best way to chart a kid's progress, as it provides real physical evidence that they're getting stronger—even if they don't see the rippling muscles that kids crave. In fact, with most weight training programs, as a way to measure one's increasing strength, the trainer will give the youngster a chart on which they write down their various exercises and how much they've lifted. It's the best way to map out their individual progress.

Ultimately, tell your youngster to be patient. Weight training involves dedication and a long-term commitment. But in the end, they'll definitely see a big difference in their bodies, and in their proficiency for the various sports they play.

CHAPTER FIVE:
What to Do If Your
Athlete Has a Bad Coach

Back in the 1950s and 1960s, it was a given that coaches always knew what was best for any athlete on their team. Whether it involved giving tips on the proper technique on how to throw a curveball, or dealing with issues of team discipline, or explaining how to develop muscles through weight training, the coach's word was the ultimate advice. And once a coach's advice was handed down to an athlete, those words of wisdom were never challenged by anyone—especially not the athlete or their parents.

But something changed over the last 20 or 30 years. Gradually, the coach's sacred words of advice have been questioned, debated, and in many cases, flat out challenged. No longer, it seems, are coaches at any level in sports allowed to give their athletic advice as if it were the gospel. If a coach makes a suggestion, or asks an athlete to try something new, or even merely wonders out loud whether an athlete might be better suited to a new approach, then the coach knows instinctively that more times than not, he or she is going to be asked why.

Are there any surveys or polls that show how strong this new trend is? No, there aren't. But I can assure you from my own experiences as both a college head coach and professional-level coach that today's generation of young athletes have been raised by their parents to ask questions if they aren't certain of a coach's—not to mention teacher's—instructions. This is not to suggest that the old way was better or worse; this is just to give notice that there's been a real sea change in the way coaches and their athletes communicate.

For example:

"Coach, are you sure you want me to switch from quarterback to tight end? I mean, I've always been the quarterback on every team I've ever played on. . . ."

"Coach, I really don't want to do the backstroke. I much prefer swimming freestyle. . . ."

"Coach, I don't think that technique of fielding a ground ball is going to work for me. . . ."

Sample questions like these pop up every day in gyms, pools, fields, courts, and rinks all over the world. Today's coaches now expect these challenges, and the smart coaches know full well how to respond to them—with well-prepared answers that make sense to the youngster. In effect, handling such questions has become part of the coach's daily teaching routine.

However, such questioning isn't the end of the story. Today, there are plenty of occasions in which coaches are pushed even stronger by kids on even larger issues. What today's coaches are not yet accustomed to hearing is a whole set of new questions, like these:

"Coach, I don't want to play midfield . . . besides, on my travel team, I play only forward. Why should I have to switch here?"

"Coach, I tried that new batting stance you taught me the other day. But my personal hitting trainer told me that approach just won't work for me. . . ."

"Coach, you know that new way you showed me of how to skate backwards? Well, I showed my Dad, and he played college hockey, and he told me that new method was all wrong. . . ."

It's one thing for the athlete to ask reasonable questions about certain issues; but pity the poor coach when the kid comes back with a conflicting opinion from his or her travel team coach, or their personal trainer, or their parent! Understandably, today's coaches don't want to be under the constant microscope from outside influences who urge the young athlete to challenge the coach's advice. After all, without a real sense of allegiance and loyalty to the team and to the coach by each team member, it's impossible for any coach to run a truly tip-top team.

But in today's ever-changing world of competitive youth athletics, this is precisely what is happening. Let's be honest: it's hard enough for a school coach to try and win games these days; it's even harder when the kids on the team are likely to challenge any coaching suggestions or directives that he or she might give! No wonder the turnover rate of high school coaches leaving the ranks is at an all-time high!

And here's another horrible—yet often unspoken—reality that plagues amateur athletics everywhere. While the majority of coaches today are wonderful, giving, and knowledgeable, and full of great tips and suggestions for the kids on their team, the sad truth is that there are an awful lot of other coaches who really aren't well versed in their sport or in the coaching trade. They don't know the best techniques to suggest, and to make matters even worse, they may not be very good at working with kids. Or they don't know how to motivate today's athletes. Or they aren't very good at communicating. Or they just aren't very sympathetic to the kids in their struggle to get better. In short, they are bad coaches; and sadly, they do exist.

Before I go any farther down this path, let me first explain that for years I have always defended coaches. Being a longtime member of the coaching fraternity, the last thing I ever wanted to do was break ranks with my coaching brethren. Yet as the years have passed, I have found that I can no longer shield my eyes to the various kinds of coaching abuses that I have witnessed.

This is not to say that I was always a perfect coach. Indeed I surely wasn't. But I do know that I never publicly humiliated or berated one of my players, nor did I ever try to outclass or embarrass the opposing team. I treated the umpires and officials with respect at all times, and I always did my best to get all of my players into the games.

But times have changed. Over the last 10 years, I have personally seen a small but growing percentage of high school and travel team coaches openly humiliate players and other teams, show a total lack of sportsmanship for the refs and officials, let talented players rot on the bench, show no sensitivity to the less-talented players on the squad, and on and on. For these coaches, it certainly appears that perhaps they're in the wrong line of work. Problem is, it's your kid who is going to suffer from their misguided coaching style.

Are bad coaches on the rise in this country? Again, no one knows, and there is probably no way to measure such a statistic. But ask yourself this: **Has your child ever played on a team where the coach was, quite simply, not very good?** Either the coach didn't know the game, or didn't know how to communicate properly with kids, or didn't know how to teach techniques, or just didn't care about sportsmanship, or all of the above. From my perspective, chances are that it's the very rare athlete in America who has never played for at least one or two bad coaches through their youth sports career.

How do I know this? Because of all the questions I'm asked when I give speeches, or when I do my sports parenting radio show, or when I receive email, invariably it's a question that starts off with "My son plays for a coach who . . ." and then the parent describes in detail the poor coaching style of their kid's coach.

A Lesson from Home

My own son's athletic experience tends to be typical of most young athletes today. When he was in high school, he played for not one, but *three* bad coaches. One coach flat-out lied to the players on the team. He would tell the kids whatever they wanted to hear, just so long as they stayed in line in practice. So if that meant, for example, promising a youngster more playing time in a game, the coach would do just that.

However, if the playing time never materialized and the kid anxiously questioned him, the coach would apologize and promise to do a better job of getting the kid more time in the upcoming games. Then, of course, the extra playing time never happened—again. By the time the kid got up enough courage to ask the coach one more time, the season would be more than half over, and the coach would simply say, "Look, I can't make any promises." This kind of response from the coach would, of course, totally devastate any youngster.

Another coach taught improper techniques to my son. My boy and his teammates instinctively knew that the coach was off base, but like good soldiers, they did what the coach asked. When the coach (and his techniques) was finally confronted by a professional, the coach backed down and was forced to change his ways. But it was clear to all the players on the team that the coach simply didn't know anything about the inner aspects of the sport and its techniques. From that point on, the kids were clearly reluctant to try anything he offered or suggested.

Another coach who my son played for was an absolute "old school" strict disciplinarian. There's nothing wrong with that kind of approach, but problems quickly began to arise when a rule was broken and the coach handed out the punishment. Invariably every infraction, large or small, was met with the same kind of penalty—a game suspension. It got to the point where usually five or six players were suspended for every game, regardless of the severity (or lack thereof) of their wrongdoing.

This kind of coaching inflexibility and non-communication ultimately led to a disastrous and disheartening season for all involved. The kids quickly felt that they couldn't talk with the coach, and the coach didn't reach out in any way to facilitate any two-way communication. As a result, a talented team marched through a miserable season, all because the coach refused to be somewhat flexible in the way he handed out punishments.

The Parental Rules of Behavior

So what does all of this mean to you?

Quite simply, if your son or daughter ever finds themselves in a situation where the chemistry between them and their coach is not positive or healthy, there are some guidelines to bear in mind—rules that you as the sports parent should share with your youngster:

Rule #1: Immediately tell your kid to keep his or her mouth shut. Kids like to complain about their teachers and their coaches to other students and athletes. But that kind of gossip invariably finds its way back to the coach. Instruct your child that if he or she wants to complain about their situation on the team, or if they want to complain about their coach, then they should only do so at home and only in front of their parents— never in front of other parents or other teammates.

Explain to them that nothing good will come of their complaining to their teammates or friends at school. In fact, only bad things can ensue when such negative thoughts are vented to others. Yes, they will be tempted to complain—that's why it is crucial for you to sit down with your child and explain how and why they should keep their mouth zipped.

Rule #2: Right after that lecture, tell your athlete to understand this fact: **the coach is still the coach**. Because of that reality, he or she still automatically deserves the respect that comes with the position. Now, your athlete might have a hard time respecting a bad coach, but it's up to you to make certain that this is enforced. Explain to your child that he or she doesn't have to be the coach's best friend, and for that matter, they don't even have to like the coach at all. But they still have to give the coach the respect that comes with the position. That means the athlete must work hard in practice, always do what the coach says, hustle all the time, and in short, do everything they're supposed to do as a young athlete. It may be difficult for the youngster to do so, but this is all part of learning to deal with frustration in life.

Rule #3: Get your athlete to clearly pinpoint their problem with the coach. Have your child explain to you what their precise issue is with the coach. Once the problem is laid out, ask your son or daughter if they have a plan or strategy that might change or influence the coach's opinion. This provides the athlete the opportunity to learn how to deal with the adversity that's confronting them. It also gets them to start thinking how they can handle these and other issues on their own, rather than having to rely upon Mom or Dad to solve their problems in life.

Rule #4: Where *your* relationship with the coach is concerned, start with this premise: **if you ever cross the line of making the coach into an enemy, you have taken a step that cannot be erased.** That means that if you angrily confront the coach about your kid, or you complain about the coach to the school's athletic director, or you grouse about the head coach to one of his assistants, or you register your concerns with the local newspaper, then you have to understand that your kid will suffer the brunt of your actions.

The much more sane approach is **never to lose your temper with the coach,** but to always address him or her in a manner of cooperation—never confrontation. Compare these two different approaches by angry parents in talking with their kid's coach:

Parent #1: *"Coach, you really have no idea what you're doing to my son. You rarely play him, and when you do, you play him in a position that's foreign to him. Don't you see how unfair that is?"*

If you were the coach here, you would immediately recoil from this parent's vicious accusation. And being human, you almost assuredly wouldn't try to help the kid out in any way.

Now, here's another parent who is just as angry as Parent #1, but tries a more cooperative approach with the coach:

Parent #2: *"Coach, I'm hoping you can help my son with a problem that's really bothering him. As you may know, he's not getting much time in the games. He understands that's your call. But he feels frustrated because he can't show his best stuff to you because he's playing in a new position. I'm sure you understand his concern . . . can we talk about this a bit?"*

This may sound so simple, but too few parents understand this common sense approach. They get so worked up about how they want to throttle the coach that they lose any semblance of civility. After all, coaches are still teachers. You wouldn't want to confront a teacher with rage in your eyes, so you have to give the coach the same kind of respect (refer to Rule #1 above).

Do these rules work? Sometimes. And no, they won't eliminate the very first issue—that you feel your kid is playing for a bad coach. But there is one promise I will make: if you follow these rules, **you'll find that your child's experience with the so-called bad coach at least has the hope of perhaps having a happy ending**. But by the same token, if you cross the line from friendly parent to angry parent, there's no way your child is going to have a chance.

Dealing with Parents: The Coach's Perspective

Too few parents understand—or for that matter, even care about—the coach's point of view. That's unfortunate, because of course it's the coach who has the power to control the kid's playing time, development, and so on. Even worse, some parents are so totally focused on their kid's rise as a star player that they let themselves fall into the trap of seeing the coach only as a bad guy. That is, the parents ask each other: "What's wrong with this coach? Why can't he see that my kid is a star player?"

In order to avoid this kind of singular vision, I often ask parents to try and put themselves in the coach's shoes. Ask yourself: is it possible that the coach actually is being fair and objective in the evaluation of your son or daughter? Is it possible that your star athlete really hasn't played all that well in practice sessions, and as a result, that's why the coach isn't as impressed with your kid as you think they should be? Are there any other reasons that might explain the coach's position regarding your child?

Parents really need to ask these hard questions of themselves; otherwise, they do run the risk of seeing their kid through a clouded lens. But assuming that you can answer all these questions objectively, and you're still convinced that the coach is not getting the job done right, you're going to have to think about perhaps having a sit-down face-to-face conversation with the coach.

Coaches, as you might imagine, don't usually like these kinds of confrontations. There's normally a reflexive reaction by coaches to defend their actions, and to that end, some coaches may even decide that they don't want to meet with any parents at any time during the course of the season.

That's an unfortunate position for a coach to take. Like any educator, they should be available during certain hours of the week where a parent or a player can meet with them. If you do decide to make an appointment with the coach, it's essential to remember what the coach brings to the session. Whatever your concern may be with the coach, understand that **the coach will always abide by these basic ground rules:**

• They won't talk about other kids on the team.

• They won't make any promises about more playing time for your kid.

• They won't respond in any way to a parent who is either angry, out of control, or threatening in any way.

• They should be forthcoming as to any concerns or complaints they have regarding your child's behavior, attitude, development, etc.

• They should be able to recap at the end of the meeting exactly what points have been covered.

As a coach myself, I have no problem being direct and honest with a parent about their child's sports career. However, I do hope that as a human being I am at least somewhat sensitive to the parents and their feelings; after all, we're talking about their child here, and parents are instinctively very protective of their kids.

A new and effective way of setting up communication lines with parents is for the coach to give out his or her email address to the parents, and urge the parents to contact the coach through that channel. First off, emails don't intrude on the coach's personal time. Secondly, and more importantly, communication is usually more accurate via email rather than through personal face-to-face or telephone conversations. Finally, emails usually don't allow emotions to seep into the discussion—and that's good.

Listen Carefully to What the Coach Says

The reason why I recap every conversation with parents at the end is because I want to make sure that the parents have really heard what I have said. We know that parents often only hear what they want to hear, so it's essential that I reinforce the real message I'm trying to get through to them. This is very important because miscommunication is almost a definite constant between hopeful parents and pessimistic coaches. Here's an example of a typical communication breakdown:

What the coach said to the parents: "If your son continues to work hard, stops goofing off so much, and makes significant progress during the practice sessions, then yes, I think he'll have a chance of getting more time in the games down the road."

What the parent heard: "Good news. Your child is going to get more playing time."

This is a fairly obvious example, but as a parent, you have to be very careful as to what the coach is **really** saying. In fact, if the coach doesn't recap the highlights of the conversation, then you should take the initiative and recap the discussion for him or her. It's essential to make sure that everybody is communicating on the same wavelength. Otherwise, even more problems are sure to crop up down the road.

So What's the Bottom Line?

First and foremost, understand that not every coach that your kid plays for is going to be cut from the same cloth as John Wooden or Joe Torre. Some coaches are great, some are terrible, and most are somewhere in the middle. That's just the law of averages. But if you truly feel that the coach is not making the sport fun or educational for your son or daughter, you certainly have options, even if they are limited. The first thing to do is to separate your good options from the bad.

For example, if the coach in question is the high school varsity coach, it certainly would not be a wise choice to demand that the school hire a new coach. That's an uphill battle that is rarely worth pursuing. As an alternative, assuming that you cannot communicate effectively with this coach, perhaps your child can play on an outside team, such as a travel team, where they can sidestep the high school program and the high school coach entirely. Or maybe your son or daughter can choose to play another sport in school for that one season. For example, when my son was a senior in high school, rather than play for a terrible baseball coach in the spring, he opted to run on the track team where he learned from a wonderful coach and built up his speed. Along the way he was still able to continue his baseball by playing for a local semi-pro team in the spring.

Did he miss playing baseball in his senior year of school? Sure. But he also knew that playing for a bad coach would have made his last semester in high school a miserable one, and as such, he was creative enough to decide to run track and play baseball outside school. Overall, it was the right decision for him.

When it comes to you and your child, I always tell parents to approach each season on an individual basis. As I mentioned at the start of this chapter, yes, there are some bad coaches out there. That doesn't mean your child has to play for them. But it does mean that you and your child will need to spend some time, do some research, and most of all, find the personal courage to sidestep that bad coach in order to seek out a program where your son or daughter will have a good coach, one who will enable them to learn and have fun while playing their respective sport.

WHAT ABOUT HIRING A PRIVATE COACH?

In recent years, more and more sports parents have inquired about the possibility of hiring a private coach or tutor for their young athlete. These coaches—most of whom charge anywhere from $30 to as much as $75 an hour or more for private instruction—normally will work with youngsters on a particular aspect of their game, or a certain skill, that may need some refining.

For example, a personal batting coach might spend an hour with the young athlete working exclusively on his batting stroke. A specialist in basketball might spend the session focusing on the kid's ability to dribble the ball with either hand. A private coach might work with a soccer goalie in developing their quickness.

These private sessions usually are done only once a week, and depending on how much the parents want to spend, can be just one session or several sessions. The age of the kids who receive such private training can range from as young as 9 or 10 to kids in their late teens.

The ultimate question is this: Do these sessions pay off?

The answer depends on whom you talk to. Most kids sense that, if nothing else, they have had the chance to truly concentrate on one facet of their game, and even better, when they actually see some improvement, the emotional payoff in terms of heightened self-esteem and self-confidence is huge.

That, for most athletes and their parents, is well worth the time and the expense of the lessons.

The only real question is whether or not the private coach you have hired really knows their sport. Since this is a new cottage industry, and no private coach has to be certified by any licenses, laws, or regulations, anyone can hang out a shingle, or send out a flyer, and say that they're eminently qualified to serve as a private coach.

This is why it's important to do a little research before you start writing checks for a private coach. Even if they have a nice brochure that details their own athletic or coaching experience, it wouldn't be a bad idea to spend a little time (on the internet or on the telephone) to see whether his or her resume checks out. For example, in many cases, parents with kids who play soccer are thrilled when a prospective private coach—especially a coach with a foreign accent—says that he played pro soccer overseas. Unfortunately, sometimes these claims are exaggerations. And what's worse, sometimes the coach—even if he did play pro ball elsewhere—may not be very good at working with young players. Of course, one of the best ways to check out a coach's credentials is by calling some of the players with whom he's worked in the past.

What kinds of expectations should you have?

Well, if you feel that hiring a private coach is going to truly transform your Little Leaguer into a Major League prospect, then you're just not being realistic. Every coach will tell you that's not to be expected. But if you simply want your youngster to get some specialized help in a particular aspect of his or her sport, then it's probably a very good idea.

Should my youngster tell his or her regular coach we're hiring a private coach?

In some cases, the high school coach will actually tell a

young athlete to go out and try to find a coach to work with them on their individual skills. But in my experience, most of the time the high school coach may resent a player who seeks tutoring instruction by someone outside the high school coach's personal system. Here's a potential conversation to illustrate what I mean:

High School Coach: Why the heck are you dribbling the ball like that? Who taught you to change your style?

High School Hoopster: Well, I've been working with a private coach, and he told me that it's better to dribble in this manner. . . ."

High School Coach: Oh yeah? Well, that private coach is flat out wrong . . . and if you want to keep doing it his way, well you can go and play on his team. But if you want to play on my team, then I suggest you do it my way."

This kind of fractious interaction can occur, so if your son or daughter does use an outside private coach, be sure to remind them to be diplomatic when discussing such matters with their current high school coach.

The bottom line on private coaches?

Yes, of course they can be a great help to a young athlete, especially if the child wants to spend some extra time on a specific aspect of their game. It's just prudent to be careful when choosing a private coach, and to be careful not to upset your high school coach.

CHAPTER SIX:
The High School Years

As a sports parent today, you're probably somewhere in your 30s, 40s, or 50s—and maybe even older. But whatever your age, it's a pretty good bet that you grew up in the 1960s, 70s, or 80s.

You must always bear that in mind, because no matter what year you graduated from high school, varsity sports in schools today have changed dramatically from the time you were in school. Think about this: routine, everyday terms and concepts that are taken for granted these days never even existed when you and I were growing up. Think back to your high school days: Can you recall ever hearing such terms as the Internet, cell phones, instant messaging, satellite dishes, AIDS, channel surfing, new recreational drugs like Ecstasy, and on and on? In addition, traditional disciplinary measures at the high school level have been replaced with student/parent contracts called "Code of Conducts," which usually stipulate that a student-athlete has to behave or else runs the risk of being dismissed entirely from a team. And how has it all changed for the coaches? Consider this: coaches today not only have to try and win games, but they also have to fend off an army of overbearing sports parents who want to know why their child isn't getting more playing time, or why they're not on the All-Star team, or why they weren't named as a captain, or how the coach plans on getting their kid recruited.

Yes, kids in the early twenty-first century still play varsity sports with great enthusiasm. But beyond that, a good deal of the surrounding environment has changed dramatically. And it's changed dramatically from three different perspectives: the parent's, the coach's, and the student-athlete's. As you guide your athlete through their high school years—from the time they first try out for the team in the 9th grade until their final game as a senior—bear in mind that the same road map you used as a high school athlete is not going to help your son or daughter in today's world.

To illustrate just how much the experience has changed, here's a basic comparison of then versus now.

Then vs. Now

THEN: A serious high school athlete should avoid the weight room at all costs. Lifting weights can add too much bulk to any aspiring athlete, and can only ruin their coordination.

NOW: It's the very rare serious high school athlete who's not involved in weight training. And if your youngster is not involved in weight training, he or she should start right away.

THEN: Only those varsity athletes who are actually starters on the team, along with a handful of key reserves, receive school varsity letters at the end of the season. The kids who spent most of the season sitting on the varsity bench may receive a certificate of participation, but not a letter.

NOW: Every kid on the varsity squad, regardless of how much playing time they received during the season, gets a varsity letter.

THEN: The high school varsity coach has the final word on all matters of discipline. If a kid breaks the rules, it's up to the coach to determine what that kid's disciplinary punishment will be—and no one ever questions that decision.

NOW: Most high schools have a Code of Conduct or Code of Behavior which the student athlete signs before the season begins. By signing, the athlete promises to abide by all the rules that the coach and team put forth. The punishments for breaking these rules, however, often tend to be lenient, and in most cases, an athlete or their parent can always appeal a punishment to the school athletic director.

In some communities in the United States today, such as in Tucson, Arizona, certain schools let varsity athletes write a Code of Conduct for *parental* behavior. That is, the kids mandate how they want the parents to act at their high school games.

THEN: Up until 1972, the only athletic activities that high school girls could participate in were basketball, field hockey, and cheerleading.

NOW: Thanks to Title IX, girls can compete in a variety of sports in school, and they are heartily encouraged to do so.

THEN: The high school varsity represents the very best level of competition for an athlete in school. Nothing else comes close.

NOW: Increasingly, talented athletes who play on travel teams instinctively know that playing for their high school team is truly a step down on the ladder of competition. Travel teams for kids 18-and-under, in most cases, offer much better competition than school teams. However, not all varsity athletes these days are good enough to make a travel team in their sport.

THEN: If you were a high school junior and senior and dreamed of playing sports in college, then you mailed letters to various colleges along with some newspaper clippings of your achievements in sports, and maybe even a letter of recommendation from your high school coach or athletic director. That almost always prompted some sort of response from the college coach.

NOW: Most top colleges start recruiting high school prospects when the kids are in 9th or 10th grade. College coaches today use network recruiting services, go to "invitation only" showcases to observe prospects, and communicate primarily with travel team coaches (as opposed to high school coaches). They rarely have time to respond personally to a letter or phone call from a high school senior. At best, that senior will receive a form letter from the college coach.

Welcome to the Twenty-first Century of High School Sports

I think you get the idea. The purpose of this little THEN versus NOW exercise is to reinforce to you the fact that the landscape of high school varsity sports has changed significantly since you and I were in school. And as tempting as it might be to use our own high school sports experience as a starting point with our own children, it really doesn't make much sense to do that.

I mentioned a moment ago that there are three distinct perspectives of high school sports: the parent's, the coach's, and the student-athlete's. Let me clarify exactly what I mean by this, because it's important to have a sense of how each party views high school sports.

The Parent's Perspective

If you are like many sports parents, chances are you have been involved in your son or daughter's sporting career since they were 4 or 5. That includes everything from making certain they're registered for youth leagues, to making sure they have the right and proper equipment, to serving as a chauffeur to all their practices and games, to finding out about summer sports camps, and so on. Even more than just taking care of the daily errands, you've also served as your child's number one booster—always there for them if things weren't going their way, lending them plenty of support and praise, and in some cases, actually serving as their private coach.

In short, you've been there for your kid every step of the way. And now that they are entering into their high school years—which is supposed to be the culmination of all of those previous years of hard work and training—you want to make absolutely certain that everything falls into place.

This is a very natural and normal way for any parent to feel. Hey, it's no secret that sports parents want their child to excel on the athletic fields of competition. They know that their child has worked long and hard to earn their athletic stripes, and they want their child to have their moments of glory during their high school years. And if their child does well enough in high school sports that they might have the chance to earn an athletic scholarship, or at least help enhance their chances for admission into the college of their choice, well, again, this is all fine.

But as one climbs the pyramid of athletic competition, as we know, getting to the top of the pyramid becomes tougher and tougher as one gets older. For most athletic kids, it's easy to be one of the stars at the elementary school level. It's a little tougher in middle school, but again, one's natural superior talent is quickly recognized by all. But once a child enters the 9th grade and starts trying out for high school sports teams, the parent has to understand that your gifted athlete is now going to have more of a challenge than ever before in maintaining their climb up that athletic pyramid.

For starters, most kids have grown up playing within their own age bracket. Whether they're playing soccer or tennis, baseball or lacrosse, they've been exposed to competing only against other athletes the same age as they are (i.e. 12-and-under soccer, 14-and-under football, etc.). However, upon arriving in 9th grade, if they truly want to make the varsity squad, many times that means competing against kids who are significantly older, bigger, and more physically mature. In most school systems, kids who are in 9th grade can try out for the varsity, but they must realize that the varsity is open to students in 9th, 10th, 11th, and 12th grades.

While that may sound very obvious to you as a sports parent, you have to understand that a typical 14-year-old is just not going to be anywhere near as physically big or strong, or as mentally or emotionally mature, as a 17- or 18-year-old. And yet, to make the varsity team, that's what your child is going to compete against. (Yes, I know there are certain sports where there are exceptions to this rule, such as swimming, gymnastics, and perhaps golf, but for the most part, the age-size factor is more the rule than the exception.)

As such, be careful as a parent not to lose your sense of perspective on your child's progress as a freshman. If nothing else, just being the new kid on the block in high school is tough enough; having them feel that they have to make the varsity as a 9th grader on top of that is usually placing much too much pressure on them.

There's another major factor that's involved in this process. If your child is trying out for the varsity, remember that the coach of the high school team is usually an educator on the high school staff (and often a member of the physical education staff). In most schools, public and private, teams are not coached by a volunteer parent or by a travel team coach who may or may not be an educator. No matter what their background may be, the high school coach is always employed by the school district, and he or she reports to the athletic director, the superintendent, and the school board. They do not report in any way back to you, the parent! That's not their job, and it's certainly not part of their official job description.

And while it would be very nice if the high school varsity coach went out of his or her way to find the time to talk with you about your son or daughter on a regular basis, you must understand that their time is very limited and that giving personalized attention to you and your youngster is not really one of their top priorities.

Again, this may all seem very obvious, but in the case of many sports parents, for some reason they have a difficult time seeing the difference between a travel team coach and a high school coach. So again, let me make this clear: **A high school coach works for the school district; they do not work for you or your kid.**

In a roundabout way, you could argue that your school taxes go to help pay these coaches' salaries—but that's a long way around. In contrast, when your child plays on a travel team, chances are you pay a certain fee directly to that coach so that your child can play on his or her team. In effect, **you are directly paying that travel coach's salary, and yes,**

because of that direct service, they should report to you. As a result, if you want to know how your child is progressing, or you want the coach to spend a little more time working with your athlete, you have every right to call the travel coach at home and ask for that kind of special attention.

This is not the case with high school coaches. Yet some parents don't see the difference. And if you are one of those parents who don't see the difference, then you run the risk of branding yourself as a "potential troublemaker" or "meddler" with your kid's high school coach, even before the kid has had a chance to prove their skills and/or make the team. That kind of label is not going to help your child's chances with the school coach.

As a sports parent who wants their child to succeed at the varsity level, **your best approach is to treat the varsity coach in much the same way that you treat your child's teachers: in a cordial yet professional way.** Keep your distance, especially early on in the year. Once the coach has had a chance to see your child perform, and has had a chance to see how your child fits into the mix of other athletes, then you can ask for a short meeting. But early on, just hang back and let the coach have the freedom to do their job.

One more note: as your child graduates from middle school to high school, remember that graduation represents a significant rite of passage for him or her. It represents a transition from being a fully dependent kid in elementary school to being a young student-athlete who can start to stand on their own two feet in high school.

And for you, Mom and Dad, you have to understand that this rite of passage has an emotional impact upon you as well. After all, your little athlete is heading off to high school, where there are no guarantees about their future in sports, and even more daunting, they're going to have to learn how to stick up for themselves, in regard to both their coaches and their teammates. This is a vitally important lesson for any athlete to learn, and the high school years are where this lesson is really absorbed.

The Coach's Perspective

The high school coach (and this would include *all* coaches—varsity, junior varsity, and freshman coaches, all in the employ of the local school district) most assuredly looks at your child in a different way than you do. As mentioned, the high school coach does not have to report to you and probably has totally different priorities than you do.

For example: Let's say your child was good enough to make the varsity squad, but she's one of the younger kids on the team and is definitely not one of the starters. However, you still would very much like your child to at least get some playing time in every game. The truth is, you just know that if your kid doesn't get in much it's going to be a source of frustration and irritation to both you and your youngster.

But from the coach's perspective, his priority is to win every game, and along those lines, he's going to let only the best players on the team play, and they're going to play a lot. This is, of course, not a problem if the coach sees your kid as one of the best players and thus plays her a lot. But if there's a difference between your opinion and the coach's opinion, your kid is going to sit on the bench. And in truth, there's not much you can do about it, because it's the coach who has the final say on playing time—not you or any other parent.

Such parental disappointments can become particularly vexing if you truly believe your freshman daughter is more talented than one of the other starters on the team. Or, in your opinion, the coach is inexplicably playing an older but less talented player a lot more than your freshman. Or if you sincerely think that the high school coach is playing your child in the wrong position. Or if the high school coach is instructing your child to make a play in a certain way, when you know that your child has been taught how to make that particular play in a totally different way by her travel team coaches.

All of these scenarios are common predicaments for sports parents, and parents scratch their collective heads as to what to do. They wonder if they should approach the coach and try to convince him that he's making a mistake in playing their kid as a midfielder when they're better suited to playing forward. Or if they should try to convince the coach that their child is infinitely more talented than the kid who's starting ahead of them.

But **today's coaches know all about parents.** Indeed, one high school coach told me recently that the number one topic of concern for coaches these days is how to cope with meddling Moms and Dad. Coaches already know that you have spent a good chunk of your life over the last 10 years trying to polish your kid into becoming a star athlete. And while coaches are sensitive to this issue, it doesn't mean that they need any help from you on how to coach their kid, or for that matter, the rest of the kids on the team.

Furthermore, high school coaches rarely want to become a parent's new best friend. In other words, some parents try to become very "buddy-buddy" with high school coaches in the hope that they will ingratiate themselves, and thus, their child will benefit somehow from this friendship. Today's coaches are too savvy for this kind of manipulative maneuvering by parents. In fact, many veteran coaches will openly tell the players on the team to remind their Moms and Dads that if they want to talk to the coach, that they have to make an appointment through the phys-ed office. The coaches will simply not make time for a spontaneous meeting with any parent either at a practice or after a game.

The Key Catch Phrases that Coaches Dread

Now, coaches will never tell you this to your face, but in their fraternity, there are certain sentences that come out of parents' mouths that immediately send off red flares as dire warnings to coaches. Here's a sampling of those parental statements that make all coaches wince:

• *"Coach, I just want you to know that my wife and I are thrilled that our 9th grader is now playing for you. The truth is, he had some really bad coaches in the middle school who just didn't know how to work with him. . . ."*

• *"Coach, we're having a family barbecue this coming weekend—it's just family and a few friends—we'd love to have you come over and join us. . . ."*

• *"Coach, I noted in the scrimmage the other day that you had Cheryl playing defense . . . you should know that she's always played offense on all of the travel teams she's played on; that's really her best position. . . ."*

• *"Coach, my kid has played on travel teams all of his life, and he's had some really good travel coaches. If you like, I could call his travel coach and perhaps have him come over and run a skills clinic or two for you and your team. . . ."*

• *"Coach, my kid has made All-Star teams in every league he's played in since he was in third grade. . . ."*

Parents, it's not that your comments are wrong or inaccurate; it's just that high school coaches don't like to have anyone in any way encroach upon their turf. They feel that they know their sport, that they know how to evaluate talent, that they are fair in their evaluations, that they know how to motivate young athletes, that they know what it takes to put together a winning team, and more importantly, that they really don't need any help from a parent.

As such, the first time you approach a coach with some introductory comments like those above, the coach will probably smile, give you a few minutes, thank you for your input, and then make a mental note to avoid you at all costs for the rest of the season. They would just prefer that you trust them to do their job, and leave them alone to do it.

All that being said, sometimes, as a parent, you do have to talk with the coach. So what's the best way to do this? Most coaches want to be treated as a professional educator. As such, in much the same way that you would call a math or English teacher for an appointment about a problem your child has in school, you can call a coach for an appointment. If your request for an appointment occurs during the season, call the coach and leave a message that emphasizes two points:

• You're most apologetic, but you need to talk with him or her about a specific concern regarding your kid; and

• You know the coach is very busy, so perhaps he or she could suggest a couple of times during the day or evening where they could squeeze you in for a few minutes.

Of course, leave your phone numbers, and if you don't hear back from them within three days, call again and leave another message. Don't worry—the coach will call back. Just make sure your schedule is flexible enough to be available when the coach has the time to see you.

So why are there occasional disparities in philosophy between high school coaches and parents? Most simply, because the coach has the team's best interests at heart. He simply wants the team to win. **And sports parents, let's be honest: you have your own child's best interests at heart. That's your top priority.** That is, if you are like most sports parents, during the game, you are focusing primarily on how your kid is performing. Your own spirits rise or fall on how they are doing. Yes, of course, you want the team to win, but you also want your child to excel.

In short, that's where coaches and parents begin to differ in their view of the game. It goes to explain why you view the game totally differently from the way the coach views the game. Remember: you're emotionally consumed with your child's performance, and you focus on them in a game. After all, you want to see him or her do well.

Example: it's a close game and the score is tied. With just a couple of minutes left, the coach calls time out. Your kid has played a goodly amount of time in the game, but at this crucial moment, the coach takes him out and puts another kid into the action. As a parent, you can see by your son's body language that he's extremely disappointed that he's being substituted for during the crucial part of the game. And you, too, feel angry and frustrated—why in the world is the coach taking my kid out?

Regardless, the game continues on, and sure enough, your kid's team loses.

Later that evening, you're talking about the game with your son. "Why did the coach take you out?" you ask. "Did he give you a reason?"

"Coach said that he wanted to go with a kid who had more experience down the stretch than me," says your son, who's a talented sophomore, "so he put one of the seniors in."

Upon hearing this brief explanation, you can react to your son in one of two ways:

• *"Oh my gosh—how can the coach be so dumb? Why he doesn't he recognize—as all the folks in the stands know—that you're ten times better than that other kid. . . ."* Or,

• *"Well, that's an interesting strategy. I personally would have kept you in. If nothing else, you're a real good player and the other kid—the senior—has to come off the bench cold and play in a tight situation."*

As an adult, I would hope you can see what the appropriate comment should be here (i.e. the second one). But your son has presented you with the coach's perception of the situation, and even though you and your son certainly don't like his perception—or the substitution he made—there are probably lots of spectators at the game who would agree that the coach made a very smart move.

The point is, a coach's viewpoint from time to time will be at odds with your perspective. Even more sobering, more times than not, and whether you want to admit it or not, the coach's perspective is going to be more correct than yours. That's not to say that your perception is flawed; it's just that you're seeing the game through the skewed prism of what's the best move for your son or daughter. And that can make a big difference.

The Athlete's Perspective

Invariably, there are occasions when the student-athlete is going to be caught between the parent and the coach, and situations like this can create a real tight spot for everyone involved. Because while the parent is debating what is the best pathway for their athlete to take, the coach is seeing the situation from the perspective of deciding what is the best possible move for the team. Ironically, with all of these grown-ups trying to figure out what's best for the athlete, people rarely take the time to talk with the athlete as to what his or her perspective is.

That's usually more than a little frustrating for the student-athlete. Whereas his coach and parents are always talking about "doing the right thing" and professing that "sports teaches character" and other such platitudes, it's not too often that we let our high school student-athletes have a real say in what's right for them. That's too bad, because once you involve your youngster in the decision-making process, that's when they start to think for themselves—about what's right for them, about what's right for their team, and about what's right for their future plans.

The famous Chinese philosopher Lao-tse once observed: "If you tell me, I will listen. If you show me, I will see. If you let me experience it, I will learn."

In this day and age, when athletes are constantly held accountable and responsible for their actions, there's no reason why you shouldn't take a page from Coach Lao-tse's playbook. In other words, start getting your student-athlete to think about sports, school, their dreams, and the real world when they are just starting in junior varsity or varsity programs.

Here's a typical example of what can happen when a student-athlete is not guided in the best way:

STAR VARSITY ATHLETE: *"Coach said that there's a curfew tonight . . . we have to be home by 10 o'clock."*

PARENT: *"Well, that's certainly understandable. Tomorrow is a big game for you."*

STAR VARSITY ATHLETE: *"Yeah, that's true . . . but me and some of the guys from the team are going to hang out by the school for a bit. We'll be home soon."*

PARENT: *"Are you sure? It's already 9:30, and I'm sure the coach was dead serious about that 10 p.m. curfew."*

STAR VARSITY ATHLETE: *"Oh yeah, but it's just me and the guys. We're not going to party or get in trouble or anything—and don't worry, I'll be home by the curfew."*

One hour later. It's now 10:30 p.m. The star varsity athlete walks through the front door back at home. His parent is waiting for him.

PARENT: *"Where were you? Don't you know what time it is?"*

STAR VARSITY ATHLETE: *"Yeah, it's a little after 10. So what's the big deal?"*

PARENT: *"Well, your coach called at 10:05 to do a curfew check. He asked to speak with you—to make sure you were home."*

STAR VARSITY ATHLETE: *"You're kidding! What did you do? Did you cover for me? Did you tell him I was in the shower or asleep?"*

PARENT: *"No, I did not cover for you. I don't tell lies. I told him that you were down at the school."*

STAR VARSITY ATHLETE: *"Oh no! Was he mad? Did he say anything?"*

PARENT: *"He didn't say much, but I can tell you this—he was not very happy."*

You can just imagine what happens next. The coach has to decide whether he's going to punish this varsity athlete for missing curfew. The parent is put in a very tough spot because, as much as he wants his son to play in the big game, he also knows that the boy blew off curfew. And the athlete is now a bag of emotions. He's worried about getting benched; he's worried about letting the coach down; he's worried about facing his teammates; he's worried about his dad; and, of course, he's worried about whether this missed curfew is going to have any long-range impact on his college scholarship dreams.

This is just the kind of situation that is played out in high schools and homes all over the country. And it's just the kind of situation where if only the student-athlete had been taught how to be more accountable for his or her actions, then he would have thought first before getting involved in something that could hurt his athletic chances.

Most parents know about the usual kinds of unwise activities that high school athletes get involved in: beer parties, driving too fast, getting in fights, destroying others' property, missing curfew, etc. To me, a lot of these problems could be eliminated if only parents would spend a little more time sitting down with their promising athlete to explain how much they have to risk by getting in trouble—not only in their athletic career, but also regarding their general health, reputation, and well being. Remember: if you don't talk about these issues with your young athlete, then who will? The coaches are not surrogate parents. It's not their job to raise your children. It's yours—and that's a responsibility you cannot, and should not, delegate to someone else.

"Hey, Boys Will Be Boys. . . ."

Unfortunately, too many parents accept the philosophy that "boys will be boys" as part of their parenting philosophy. Perhaps that's the way they were raised by their own parents when they were teenagers. But regardless of where or how these sports parents got that philosophy, it's still wrong in today's world.

Example: On a warm sunny spring day in 2002, there was a power failure at Harrison High School in suburban Harrison, NY. All of the kids were dismissed from school at mid-day. Seizing upon their unexpected day off from school, a bunch of high school athletes, many of them football players, congregated at a close-by home (the parents were not home) and proceeded to throw a beer party.

Unfortunately, during the course of the afternoon, there was a fight between two boys, and a punch or two was thrown. One football player was struck in the face and fell to the ground where he banged his head on the sidewalk. He was unconscious. His teammates didn't know what to do. No one called 9-1-1 for emergency help for at least 20 minutes. The struck football player lapsed into a coma, and then died in the hospital a day later.

Fast-forward six months later. Same town of Harrison, NY. Another beer party attended by high school football players. Some players got drunk. There were arguments. One of the players, a star running back, got so angry that he punched his arm through a window, causing cuts that required 40 stitches. How did the school system deal with this second beer party? Several players (about nine) were suspended for one game. Then they could play again.

I use this example not necessarily to pick on Harrison High School, which has gone through a terrible tragedy with the death of a young football player. After all, illegal underage beer parties take place in high schools all over this country. And by all accounts, it doesn't appear that is going to change. But especially if you're a sports parent, and your son or daughter is hoping to use their athletic abilities as a springboard for college or even the pro ranks, now's the time to talk with them directly about how to conduct themselves when it comes to hanging out with friends.

Tough Advice in Difficult Situations

Okay, so what do you tell your athlete?

Explain to them how hard they have worked to get where they are in sports. Explain to them that just being caught in the wrong place at the wrong time can destroy their reputation and take all of their hard work away from them.

Their response might be: *"Yeah, but I don't drink or smoke . . . it's just my friends who do that."*

Understood; and let your athlete know that his or her decision not to smoke, drink, or do drugs is to be admired. But also let your child know that if they are in attendance at these kinds of parties, then they run the risk of being found guilty by association. Explain to them that athletes—especially high school varsity athletes—tend to be a lot more visible in a community than regular students. So if another parent, teacher, police officer, or whoever comes across a bunch of high school kids at a beer party, they're most likely going to point out the star athlete more so than the other kids who were in attendance. That may not be fair, but in our sports-crazed society, people in the general community do place higher standards of conduct upon the gifted athletes.

On some occasions, your young athlete may say: *"But the parents were home. They said they would rather have the kids drink beer there—while they were home—rather than drive around and get killed."*

Explain to your son or daughter that this kind of explanation doesn't make the situation right. In fact, the parents who serve beer are then legally responsible if an underage kid gets drunk at their home and then gets hurt. Even more so than the kids' mistakes, this kind of stupid parental behavior can never be condoned. They should be reported to the local police.

Your son or daughter may rationalize their actions with a statement like: *"We're just blowing off some steam. Hey, it's Saturday night, and we just won the big game. . . ."*

Again, this is Parenting 101. Just take a few moments to remind your kid that once they leave the house, they have to be accountable for their actions in life. That's part of growing up—not just as an athlete, but as an adult. Long after their sports career is over, they have to live with themselves and whatever reputation they have built for themselves.

NUTRITIONAL SUPPLEMENTS: WHAT YOU SHOULD KNOW

Like it or not, young athletes today are bombarded by massive advertising campaigns on how they can become bigger and stronger by simply consuming some nutritional or herbal supplements. This temptation can hit high school kids pretty hard.

Chances are you've also seen the ads, which promise added muscle and bulk to anyone who commits to these planned nutritional programs. And sure enough, the vast majority of these nutritional supplements are all perfectly legal, and are routinely sold over the counter in health food stores everywhere.

So what's the problem? Or perhaps the more accurate question is: Why shouldn't a young athlete take nutritional supplements if they want to get bigger and stronger?

Let's start with creatine, which is perhaps the most popular muscle enhancer on the market today. By the time they're 12 or 13, all young athletes—male and female—see or hear that taking a hefty dose of creatine every day will quickly help them pack an extra 20 pounds of pure muscle onto their frame within a matter of weeks. For the skinny youngster who is eager to add some rippling muscles to their frame, creatine sounds like the perfect answer.

But before you let your athlete run down to the mall to buy a giant jug of the product, you ought to know all of the inherent risks that come with creatine. **For starters, creatine is not regulated by the Food and Drug Administration (FDA).** That's because it is considered, by law, to be a food supplement, and thus it's not subject to the FDA's very rigorous testing and approval process. Should this reality worry you if your child consumes the substance? Well, if you talk to the manufacturers of creatine (which, by the way, is a hefty multi-million dollar business), they will tell you that creatine has not been shown to have any adverse impact on one's health.

That claim is true to a certain degree. But the problem is that there are no long-range scientific studies available on creatine and its impact on the human body. Nobody really knows whether it is completely safe to take—or if it isn't. What medical scientists do know is that creatine is a naturally occurring protein substance in the human body. But when it is manufactured and marketed as a nutritional supplement, it is sold in a highly concentrated form. As one scientist put it: "In terms of all the extra protein you're pushing into your body, taking creatine on a daily basis is like eating 83 steaks in one sitting."

Is that necessarily bad for your son or daughter? Again, no one knows. Only now are a few studies just coming forward. One bit of research suggests that the residue of creatine in the human body eventually transforms into a formaldehyde-like substance. As you might imagine, having formaldehyde, which is used as a preservative, circulating in one's body is not healthy.

Users have found that creatine use can also result in severe dehydration. Some professional teams have actually banned their players from using creatine because of this common problem. The Miami Dolphins, for one, banned the consumption of creatine by its football players because the users would develop severe cramps when they worked out in the warm, muggy temperatures of Florida.

Finally, if your youngster intends to play sports in college, you should note that creatine use is currently banned by the NCAA. So, if your athlete is using it now, they ought to make sure to stop by the time they enroll in college, if not sooner.

But again, the real question is: Will taking creatine hurt your child's health in the long run? Until more clinical tests have been run, there's no definitive answer. However, as a parent, it certainly makes sense to have this discussion with your youngster, because athletes in their late teens always tend to focus on the present—they feel that they're going to live forever. They don't often recognize that they might want to consider their long-term health.

What About Steroids, Andro, and Ephedra?

Will anabolic steroids help your kid develop rippling muscles? Absolutely. But what about the side effects of steroids? Unlike creatine, **the dangers of steroid use are well documented by medical science**, and the long-range impact of steroids will almost certainly cause a number of problems for users. These ill effects include mental concerns such as "steroid rage" and depression, the shrinking of testicles, acne, baldness, heart problems, liver problems, and on and on.

If your son (or daughter) is talking about the positives of steroid use, be sure to immediately steer them away. Not only are steroids against the law, but the health risks can be severe.

Androstenedione—known as "andro"—is known as a precursor to anabolic steroids. Andro was first made widely known to the American sporting public during Mark McGwire's drive to break the single-season homerun record in 1998. At that time, since andro was not banned by Major League Baseball, McGwire openly used it and defended its legality to all.

But curiously, a year after McGwire broke the record, he stopped using andro. He gave no reason why he quit the substance, but clearly every article that was published in the media talked about andro's devastating effect on one's long-range health. Then, not long after McGwire's decision to stop using the substance, Major League Baseball joined the rest of the other professional leagues in finally banning andro.

Another popular substance called "ephedra," like creatine, was always considered a kind of food supplement that did not fall under the domain of the FDA. But in recent years, there have been a number of deaths in the sports world where evidence indicated that perhaps the victim had been using ephedra (a substance that speeds up the body's metabolism in order to help one lose weight very quickly). The recent death this past spring of Baltimore Orioles' pitcher Steve Bechler was linked, in large part, to his using a substance with ephedra. Steve was merely trying to lose weight in a hurry. It ended up costing him his life. The good news is that more and more states are now trying to ban the sale of ephedra-based products in stores, but as of this book's publication, ephedra is still available to all in retail outlets.

What's the bottom line where your athlete is concerned? First, note that every young athlete sees the claims on television or in magazines to improve one's strength and gain explosive power by using these kinds of nutritional supplements. Take a moment to explain to them that just because it's for sale in a store doesn't mean that it's healthy for them (remember: like other food supplements, the quality or purity of the substance is not regulated by the federal government). And tell them that there might be some very serious long-term health problems associated with the ingestion of these substances. They might not care about the potential state of their health in their 30s or 40s, but they should. And you should be the one who raises that concern.

In short, if your youngster wants to get bigger and stronger, tell them to hit the weight room. That's still the best—and safest—way to build their bodies. Supplements offer an alternative approach, but at what price to one's body?

What about Advanced Sports Academies?

In your travels with your youngster, you may hear from time to time about these exotic-sounding "schools" that specialize in sports. These schools, or "sports academies," have been around for several decades, and have traditionally catered to athletes who are either in high school or middle school, and for the most part, are lucky enough to come from families where there's enough money to finance these kids' athletic pursuits.

Some of the more famous sports-training academies have been geared towards golf and tennis. Nick Bolletieri, the famous tennis instructor, started his Florida-based academy for promising players more than 25 years ago. Thousands of kids have attended, and some of them even went on to become stars. Some of Bolletieri's distinguished alums include Andre Agassi, Jim Courier, Boris Becker, Anna Kournikova, and Monica Seles. On the golf side, David Leadbetter ran a training academy for young golfers. With the success of his David Leadbetter Golf Academy, he is known by many as the world's leading golf instructor.

But since the 1990s, both Bolletieri's school and Leadbetter's academy were taken over by the International Management Group (IMG), the well-known sports marketing agency. Today, the IMG Sports Academies in Bradenton, Florida, are perhaps the best-known in the country. They offer special instruction in tennis, golf, baseball, ice hockey, soccer, basketball, and much more.

According to a recent article in *Sports Illustrated* (November 24, 2002), the IMG Sports Academies currently have 523 boys and girls enrolled on their campus, and most of these kids are of high school age. In addition to spending as much as six hours a day working on their individual sport, the students are also tutored on nutrition, weight training, and the mental side of their sport (performance enhancement). There's also a private school nearby the campus if kids want to continue their education, and of course, many of them do.

What's curious about these sports academies is that not every kid who attends is considered to be a blue-chip athletic prospect. What is prevalent, however, are kids who are extremely motivated to make the most out of their talent. Writes Kelley King in *Sports Illustrated*: "The surprising truth about IMG Academies is that the vast majority of students, while athletic and motivated, lack the extraordinary natural ability that stamps them as potential pros. When you get down to it, the primary requirement for admission is financial ability, not athletic ability. . . ." (*Sports Illustrated*, Nov. 25, 2002, p. 53)

The cost to attend IMG and other similar academies is substantial. Again, according to *Sports Illustrated*, the "bare bones" curriculum (which includes daily sports instruction, once-a-week mental conditioning, room and board) runs about $30,000 a year. If you want your kid to attend the local private school for education, that's another $11,000, or a total of more than $41,000 per year. In other words, it's not inexpensive.

But while highly motivated athletes make for wonderful members of a team, simple high motivation doesn't translate into blue chip talent. As Dan Doyle, author of the *Encyclopedia of Sports Parenting*, writes: "Maybe the biggest positive takeaway from the academy experience is that you find out how good you really are." What Doyle is really saying is that for most kids who attend these sports academies, they find out very quickly that no matter how hard they work at their skills, they're never going to become a professional or perhaps even a top collegian in their sport. That, as you might imagine, can be a very rude awakening for any youngster (and their parents)—especially at a price tag of $30,000 a year.

In fact, sports parents with grand dreams for their son or daughter often fall into what I call the "All-American work ethic" trap. That is, for lots of parents who have been successful in their own lives, they have lived under the strong belief that the harder one works, the more successful one becomes. This strong work ethic has helped propel them in business, or in the law, or in medicine, or for that matter, in just about any profession where good ol' hard work gets the job done.

The problem is that too many of these parents apply that same All-American work ethic to their kids in sports. They truly believe if the child works hard enough at their game, then eventually all that hard work will propel them into the higher echelons of competitive athletics. Unfortunately, while hard work will raise a child's ability to a certain level, **unless there's real, God-given superior athletic talent, simple hard work and dedication will not raise a youngster to star athletic status.**

Take, for example, a superstar NBA player like Amare Stoudemire, who jumped from high school directly to the pro ranks with the Phoenix Suns. Most sports parents today would naturally assume that the 6-10, 245 lb. Stoudemire was a dominant player in the youth and travel leagues as a kid.

But they would be surprised to learn that Stoudemire did not even play any organized basketball until he was 14, and then played less than two seasons while in high school. In fact, it wasn't until his senior year in high school that he truly blossomed and was named Florida's Mr. Basketball. It was then that the NBA began to take notice.

In other words, here's a star athlete who literally bypassed all of the high-pressured competition of travel teams when he was a kid, and didn't really start to develop his God-given skills until he was well into his teenage years. And judging by his performance in the NBA, missing those early years didn't hurt his development at all. (*New York Times*, January 26, 2003)

Look at the soccer phenom Freddy Adu. Only 13 years old, he's considered to be the absolute best player for his age in the United States. In fact, the Ghana-born Adu is now starring for the U.S. national under-17 team, and is considered to be America's top rising star. For most 13-year-olds in this country, they're just hoping to make their school's middle school or travel soccer team.

But here again, Freddy was born with extraordinary athletic talent. The very first time he played in an organized basketball game (a junior varsity game at his school), he scored 28 points. The first time he played golf, on a 370-yard par-4 hole, Freddy got to the green in two strokes and two-putted for par. In other words, he was blessed with exceptional athletic ability. (*Sports Illustrated*, March 3, 2003)

"You Can't Measure a Kid's Heart"

No, you can't. But sports parents have to remember that at a certain level, perhaps the college or even high school level, the coach will always go with the more physically talented and usually physically larger kid. That simple reality is often very difficult for a parent to comprehend. "C'mon, coach," the parent will protest, "you can't measure a kid's heart—and no one works harder at football than my kid."

"Yes, that may be true," replies the football coach, "and I'm sure your son works his tail off. But the truth is, he's only 5-foot 10 inches and weighs 170 pounds. I have several kids on the team who are all over 6 feet, and all weigh over 200 pounds, and they all run faster than your son. As such, I'm sorry, but I'm going to stick with the bigger players."

The bottom line on sports academies? There's nothing wrong with doing some investigation into them for your son or daughter. Just remember that to get to the elite levels in sports, a youngster needs talent as well as drive. And talent can't be taught.

CHAPTER SEVEN:
Is Your Kid Really a College Recruit?

For most high school athletes, there are very few moments more special than getting a letter in the mailbox from a college coach—a coach who is interested in having you find out more about his or her college program. And that student's pride is shared just as much by his or her parents.

After all, what could be more impressive than hearing from a college coach? After all, for lots of parents and their kids, getting a college coach to sit up and take notice is the ultimate pay-off. So, if those letters—or better yet, a phone call—start to come in, enjoy the moment. Your son or daughter should be immensely proud of what they have accomplished in sports.

However, the next question is whether your child really does want to continue playing sports in college. While that question may be a silly one for your kid (of course they want to play!), many other kids really don't want to make the kind of commitment that's necessary to play a sport in college. For these student-athletes, the overall purpose of playing sports has been to have fun, and also to enhance their college application so that they might better their chances of getting into their first-choice school. But beyond that, they don't want to pursue athletics at the collegiate level.

All this being said, if your son or daughter does want to continue to play sports in college, it's absolutely key that you establish a very clear line of communication with the coaches of those colleges that he or she is considering. The truth is, all parents of college-bound students have to do their homework when it comes to picking a school for the next two or four years. You just can't be casual about the process, because while college recruiting is full of hopes and dreams, it's also full of dead-ends and blind alleys.

Because of all the time that intercollegiate sports require from athletes these days, you have to do even more homework than you may think necessary when it comes to having your child select a college. And by the way, it makes no difference whether your student-athlete wants to play at a Division I, Division II, or Division III program—all college programs involve a tremendous time commitment from their athletes. In fact, even though your athlete successfully handled the grueling balancing act in high school of combining school work with athletics, you need to forewarn them that the demands on them in college—especially with sports—will actually get worse, not easier.

But let's get back to choosing a college. The most important piece of the puzzle is for you to try and be objective about your son or daughter's athletic ability. Granted, that is not easy for a parent, especially a parent who has so much time vested in their child's athletic development. You should have the good parental common sense to seek out the opinions of the coaches and athletic directors who have seen your youngster perform. They should provide an objective opinion as to whether your child will have what it takes to compete at the intercollegiate level, and if so, at what level.

Through no fault of their own, very few parents have a real understanding of just how good a youngster has to be to play at the Division I level. For that matter, most parents have no idea of how good one has to be to play Division III. Why? Because for the most part, very few parents ever got beyond high school sports themselves, and as a result, they truly have no idea just how competitive college sports are these days.

Example: I once had a father approach me about his son playing college baseball. The dad told me that his son was a very good pitcher, and even had some pro scouts look at the kid. As a result, the proud papa was thinking that maybe his son should be looking at some of the premier college programs in the country, like the University of Miami or UCLA.

When I asked the dad whether he or his son had heard from the coaches at these kinds of top Division I schools, he admitted that no, they hadn't. After hearing that—mind you, the boy was already well into his senior year of high school—I suggested that the boy look at some top Division III college baseball programs instead. The father immediately scoffed at the idea: "C'mon, Division III? They don't even give out athletic scholarships! Besides, Division III baseball is just like intramurals in high school. Anybody who tries out can make the team . . . and my kid's a lot better than that!"

Undaunted, I asked the dad if he had ever seen a top Division III college baseball game. He admitted that he never had. Upon hearing that, I strongly suggested that he and his son go out and see some Division III games as soon as possible—so that he could see for himself just how good Division III baseball players really are. The truth is that most Division III athletic programs are a giant leap from any high school sports program, and if you, as a sports parent, aren't aware of that, then you're giving poor advice to your son or daughter.

What happened to the Dad and his son? Well, they did go out and watch some local Division III baseball colleges play, and indeed they were impressed with what they saw. Even better, they befriended one of the college coaches at a game, and sure enough, the boy ended up enrolled in that D-III college. For him and his father, it was a win-win situation in the end.

Just remember this: **the difference between high school sports and college sports is gigantic.** For the typical prospective college athlete, you have to be very, very honest as to where you might fit into the mix in college.

Listen Very Carefully to the Coach

Let's start with the assumption that your son or daughter has, in fact, received some sort of correspondence from a college coach. Of course, this is wonderful. If nothing else, it signifies to your son or daughter that a coach is interested enough in their athletic ability to at least reach out and contact them.

However, just getting a letter in the mail hardly makes your kid into a recruited athlete. In fact, we've often discussed the confusion surrounding college recruiting on my weekly sports parenting radio show on WFAN in New York City. On one particular show, a coach called in to suggest that the NCAA ought to set a standard rating system for all prospective college recruits. That is, he suggested that a college should tell you up front where your son or daughter ranks between 1-4, with a 1 indicating an absolutely rock-solid, full athletic scholarship recruit, and a 4 meaning that the college is only mildly interested in your son or daughter as an athlete. A 4 ranking would suggest that your child is not an active part of the coach's plans, that your kid is not going to be offered any scholarship money, and quite honestly, that he or she is seen as a fringe player who may or may not make the team.

Yet in this hypothetical ranking system—and that's just what it is at this point—being a 4 would still mean that your child might receive an occasional letter, phone call, or email from the college coach. But the standard form letter or email is still a long ways from having the college coach personally arrange an official recruiting visit on campus for your son or daughter, not to mention having a serious chat with the coach about how much scholarship money your athlete would get.

All this being said, it is still a very exciting moment for your son or daughter to receive a piece of mail from a university coach. But after the initial joy, it's then up to the student—and you, the parent—to start compiling a list of questions to ask the college coaches. **Above all, listen carefully and objectively to what the coach has to say.** Coaches speak to dozens of prospective players and their parents each year, and they are very precise and usually very non-committal about the words they use when talking with prospects and parents.

Unfortunately, too many times parents and kids, because they're excited to be meeting with the coach, will only hear those parts of the conversation that they want to hear. For example, the college coach might say, "David, it's clear that you're a great kid—just the kind of student-athlete that we're looking for here at State University—and we sure hope you'll apply here. . . ."

The 18-year-old high school student hears this, and it's music to his ears! Same goes for David's parents—they're listening to the same wonderful words! But take a step back and run through the coach's enthusiastic appeal again. You'll realize that while the coach gushes that he would love to have David enroll at State University, there was never any mention of David making the team, or for that matter, that David would even get a tryout!

Is this kind of drastic misunderstanding possible? After all, didn't the coach say to David and his parents that David's "a great kid . . . just the kind of student-athlete we're looking for . . . we sure hope you'll apply here"? Yes, he did say all those nice things, but nowhere was there any indication that David would be a starter on the team, or for that matter, would even make the team!

Sadly, this kind of drastic misunderstanding happens all the time— because the student and his or her parents are so eager to hear encouraging words of praise from the coach. (After all, chances are the kid and his parents spent the entire day or two getting to the college campus, and meeting the coach in person is the high point of the trip!) But from the coach's standpoint, he knows exactly what he is saying—and more important, what he is **not** saying to this young man and his parents.

Sadly, it's up to the parents—not the college coach—to be ready to press ahead with tough questions, and to push until they get real answers. Obviously, if the coach is defensive and guarded in his responses, or tries to avoid the questions altogether, or won't give you real answers, then you ought to seriously consider whether your son or daughter will have any chance of making the team at that college. **This realization might be disappointing, but it's certainly better to know these things now rather than later, when your kid is already enrolled in the school.** Ultimately, take comfort in the fact that there are lots of wonderful colleges out there. Do your homework during the search and decision process, and make sure you and your child feel good about the coach.

Asking the Right Questions

When you do get an interview with a coach, be sure to take notes during your conversation. And have wise questions ready to ask. Here are seven questions to keep in mind:

1. *What kind of chance does my son or daughter have to be a starter on your team?*

This is, of course, the ultimate question to ask a college coach. We'll come back to this question later on. But don't forget it, because it's the most important question of them all. That being said, it's the rare coach who will guarantee any high school prospect a starting position. But what you do want to hear is that the coach will guarantee that your child will have every opportunity to compete for the starting job, and that means plenty of playing time in practices, scrimmage games, and so on. Again, giving your kid "a good, long look" is something that the coach can, and should, promise you.

2. *"Coach, how many kids are you recruiting for my son's position?"*

If the coach is reluctant to tell you, or doesn't know, or says he doesn't work like that, be more than a little skeptical. Every college coach knows exactly how many kids are graduating, how many slots are open, how much scholarship money is available, and most importantly, who he's pinpointing to bring in as a recruit and what positions he'll be recruiting.

As such, get the coach to be as candid as possible. Say something like: "Coach, I don't have to tell you how important choosing the right college is for my kid. And playing sports is a very big part of his life. Plus there's a substantial cost in going to college. So please tell us, as best you can, where do you see my kid fitting in? And more specifically, how many other first basemen are you bringing into the program—after all, he's a first baseman and he wants to play." Listen carefully to the coach's answer, and if you are not exactly sure that you heard him clearly, ask him to say it again.

3. *"Coach, is my son (or daughter) being considered as an active recruit for you and your college?"*

This is the second most important question to ask the coach, and in some cases perhaps even the most important. Why? Because with most college coaches today, unless your son or daughter is a bona fide recruited athlete, there's very little chance of your kid ever making that college varsity team.

"Oh that's not right, Rick," I can hear you saying. "Maybe that's true for athletic recruits at Division I football or basketball programs. But at Division II and Division III colleges, even the top ones, regular college students go out for the team as just 'walk-ons' all the time and make the squad."

Maybe a long, long time ago that was true. But not today. Even at the Division III schools—or at least at the athletically competitive schools—most of the athletic teams' athletes are recruited by the coaches. These coaches know which high school athletes have a real shot at getting into their school and will help to make their team win. As such, each fall these college coaches will go to the admissions people and make a strong case to admit their slotted recruits, even if these student-athletes don't have the same kinds of grades or SAT or ACT scores that other students may have.

And this process happens everywhere—not just at the large Division I universities where having a winning football or basketball team is essential to keep the athletic coffers full. It also happens at highly academic Division III schools like Williams College and Amherst College, where the alums take great pride in having their college feature great sports teams.

In a recent front page story in the *New York Times* (Sept. 22, 2002), it was made clear by *Times* sportswriter Bill Pennington that having a kid make a college team as a walk-on just doesn't happen anymore. On many college campuses these days, the coaches don't even have tryout sessions. Or if they do, it's a one-day perfunctory tryout after which it's extremely rare that any kid is asked to stay on with the varsity.

In Pennington's article, Larry Cochell, the head baseball coach at the University of Oklahoma, is quoted as saying that he holds a one-day tryout for walk-ons during the first week of classes. Last year, 25 walk-ons tried out. How many made Cochell's team? None. In fact, it's extremely rare for a walk-on to make his club.

By the way, this is not just confined to sports like baseball or football. Warren Mandrell, the men's track and cross-country coach at Miami University in Ohio, says he routinely turns away around 30 walk-ons for his team each year. Pennington also writes of Jason Lindberg, a gymnast since he was in elementary school who enrolled at the University of Oklahoma and wished to compete for a spot on the gymnastics team. Even though he was not recruited by Oklahoma, Lindberg thought that he could do well enough to make the team as a walk-on.

But Lindberg was stunned when he was told as a freshman that no male gymnasts would be allowed to even try out for the team. Obviously, he had no chance of making the team if he wasn't even given a tryout. And indeed, he didn't.

Pennington points out that being denied the opportunity to try out for a college team is becoming more and more the norm in college athletic programs all over the country. In short, Pennington observes, "Male walk-ons have essentially become an unwanted luxury."

I recall a conversation I had with Scott Bradley, the head baseball coach at Princeton University, about recruits and walk-ons. He told me flat out that that they don't have any tryouts for walk-ons at Princeton. "Every member of my team is a recruit," says Bradley. "That's just the way it is at Princeton." In short, if your student-athlete is lucky enough to be admitted into Princeton on academic merit, even if he wants to try out for the baseball team, he most likely won't get a chance.

Unfortunately, that's the way it is with most college sports programs these days. So again, unless your kid is a real honest-to-goodness recruit (that means lots of personalized letters and phone calls from the coach, along with being invited to visit the campus), chances are he or she will scarcely get a look.

4. *Are there any exceptions to the recruit-only situation?*

Yes, there are a few exceptions. The most notable is something called the "recruited walk-on." That's typically an athlete who the college coach knows about from high school, and would like to have the athlete go to his school. But the coach is not so enthusiastic to offer the youngster any kind of athletic scholarship for his services. In other words, the coach is trying to have the best of both worlds: he welcomes the kid to enroll in his college, but the coach knows that he doesn't have to shell out any scholarship dough to entice the youngster to attend the school.

Many times, the coach might even say to the boy, "Look, I know you're a very good high school player. If you come to my school, I'll give you every chance to make the team. And if you do make it, I'll get you some scholarship money for the following year—when you're a sophomore."

From the athlete's perspective, that sounds like a fair deal. Why? Because from the athlete's viewpoint, he just knows he's going to impress the coaching staff, and he just knows that he'll make the team, and he just knows that he'll get scholarship money for the next year. **Chalk all of this up to positive—as well as very naïve—thinking.**

The sad truth is that the coach is most likely not going to keep the kid on the team, because (a) the coach is only going to pay attention to those kids whom he did give scholarship money to, and (b) the coach assumes that the kid will see for himself that he's not good enough to play at this level, and thus will quit the team all by himself.

Remember: once the practices begin, if the coach doesn't think that the boy can help the team, he can cut him without any strings attached. All the coach has to say to the frustrated walk-on is: "Sorry, son, but I don't think you're going to help our team much." And with that, the kid is cut, and his dreams dashed. It sounds cruel, but that's the state of college athletics these days.

5. *I heard that football walk-ons have a better chance of making the team. Is that true and why?*

Yes, football walk-ons do occasionally have a better chance of making a team, and curiously, this happens most notably at the large colleges where football rosters are full-size under NCAA rules. Because a college program might have as many as 90–100 players or more on its football team, the chances of a "recruited walk-on" making the squad are greatly improved simply because the size of the roster is so huge.

But here again, traditionally inspirational stories like the one told in the movie *Rudy* are very, very rare. *Rudy*, you might recall, focused on a diminutive football walk-on named Rudy Ruettiger at Notre Dame who played for four years on the back-up practice teams but finally got to play in one game—for one play—as a senior. Again, *Rudy* is a wonderful film, and is actually based on a true story, but the truth is, these kinds of happy endings only happen very, very rarely these days.

6. *Do all of these issues regarding recruits and walk-ons apply to women athletes, as well?*

According to Pennington, the walk-on situation is a little better for women at the collegiate level. For the most part, there tend to be more opportunities for female walk-ons to make college teams. Again, the recruited athletes always get the top priority, but most athletic directors will point out that it's a little easier for women to make a college team.

However, if your daughter seriously wants to continue her sports career in a college program, the same advice applies to her as it does to her male counterpart. That is, try to get the college coach to designate her as a real recruit, and even better, to get some scholarship money offered **now**—not as a stipulation of her someday making the team.

Why are there more opportunities for women? There's no real clear-cut answer, but most experts point to the impact of Title IX, a national law by which every college athletic program has to provide the same number and kind of opportunities for women athletes as they do for male athletes. While in theory that makes all the sense in the world, the reality is that since there are more males in college who want to make sports teams, it's the men who often find themselves getting cut from a team. However, the impact of Title IX is now currently being studied, as it does seem clear that in its attempt to even out the playing field for men and women in college, unexpected problems are now beginning to crop up.

7. *If the coach says, "Yes, your kid is the one I want," can I then ask about scholarship money?*

This, of course, is the best possible scenario of all. When the coach starts talking about scholarship dough, you can almost act as an agent for your son or daughter. How do you negotiate this kind of deal?

First, have everything—including all the financial numbers—written down by the coach on a piece of paper that you can take away. Make sure the coach—not you—writes the offer down. In case there's ever any misunderstanding about what was offered, it's essential to have the details of the offer written in the coach's handwriting.

Second, remember that you hold the leverage in this situation. If the coach is eager to have your son or daughter sign a letter that binds them to the school, understand that you hold all the cards here. Still, at this point, you should not sign any papers or agree to any terms until you and your athlete have had some time to digest the offer, do your own calculations, and if you want, go back and talk to other college coaches who are recruiting your kid to see if they can match the offer you have in hand.

Most coaches will not pressure you too hard on these issues because they do not want to run afoul of the NCAA recruiting rules (they and their program could be severely penalized for misrepresenting the facts or employing some other unethical tactics). They also know that most parents and their athletes don't want to feel as though they're being pressured to make a decision. The coaches will make their sales pitch, and like any good salesman, they'll give you some time to shop around and make up your mind. So whatever you do, do not panic upon hearing the first whiffs of an offer and ask for the nearest dotted line to sign.

What most sports parents don't normally understand is that college coaches have a certain amount of freedom to entice and lure student athletes into their program. For example, at a number of highly academic colleges, the coaches are granted a certain number of slots each year to bring recruited athletes into their program.

What about the More Academic Colleges?

Many recruits to the more academically inclined schools do not, quite honestly, have the grades or board scores that would normally make them attractive to the college admissions people, but because they are recruited athletes, often they will be granted admission. One admissions officer at an Ivy League school recently observed that while the overall admissions rate for high school students is as prohibitive as 1 out of 5, for recruited athletes at the same college, the rate is closer to 1 out of 2. And remember, while these are usually top high school athletes, they often don't have the necessary grades and SATs to be admitted into the college. (For a more detailed analysis of the Ivy League and its schools' athletic recruits in particular, be sure to find a copy of the book *A Is For Admission* by Michele Hernandez. As a former admissions officer at Dartmouth, she writes candidly about the "Athletic Index" and what kinds of standards the Ivy League coaches maintain to recruit athletes.)

So why would a top academic college allow this kind of recruitment of "lesser" students? Because the recruitment of top athletes theoretically will lead to better teams, and with better teams comes winning teams, and with winning teams comes more financial support from proud alumni, along with more national recognition. While this sounds a bit out of character, this is the mindset by which most Ivy League-type schools operate.

The College Athlete and Time Commitment

Now that you and your student-athlete have been considering taking the step into college athletics, let's revisit the issue of time commitment in college sports. Whether your son is playing football at Ohio State or your daughter is playing volleyball at St. Mary's, he or she (and you) are going to have to be aware that playing a sport in college demands a huge amount of time. Yes, of course your child worked hard in high school to balance their time between sports and schoolwork, but that balancing act becomes even more precarious in college.

For starters, college practice sessions are longer than high school practices. And while there are NCAA rules and regulations about how many hours a week a student can devote to team practice, there are other athletic concerns that a student must attend to outside official practices, including hitting the weight room, watching videotape, or just traveling to the next game. All of this—plus practice time—makes for an extremely demanding schedule for any collegiate student-athlete. Also—and this is really important for those athletes who may be good enough to make the college team but not the pros—the college academic course load is far more demanding and time-consuming than any high school curriculum anywhere.

As such, if your son or daughter has had some difficulty with the balancing of time management in high school, then they had better be prepared for when they get to college. College sports are a major, major commitment. And many times, the athlete has to decide for himself or herself whether the payoff is truly worth it. But again, it's better to be prepared going in, rather than realize halfway through the first semester that their grades are suffering because of long afternoons on the practice field.

CHAPTER EIGHT:
How Will the College
Recruiters Find My Kid?

There's a lot of mythology floating around about how college coaches go about recruiting kids for potential scholarships. For many sports parents and their sons and daughters, the entire process seems cloaked in mystery, and they search in vain for answers to such questions as:

• Should the student-athlete write a letter to those college coaches whose schools they are interested in?

• Should the student-athlete rely upon their high school coach to make calls and develop contacts for them?

• Should the parents put together a highlight tape of their athlete's top performances?

• Should a student-athlete pay money for a college recruiting service, which promises that their athletic profile will be sent to those colleges they're interested in?

• Should a youngster start contacting college coaches during their junior year, or wait until their senior year?

These basic questions are, of course, merely the tip of the iceberg, but they at least provide a starting point. And now, for starters, here are some basic hard truths.

It's fine to have your son or daughter write a letter to a college coach to express interest in their program. Many kids even include copies of newspaper clips highlighting their achievement of All-League or All-County status, or perhaps even some sports-page write-ups of their big

games. This is all fine, but for the most part, since college coaches literally receive thousands of letters like these, it's difficult for them to be
impressed. Joe Trainer, the defensive coordinator for the Villanova
University (Division I-AA) football team, says: "We have about 13–16
scholarships each year, and each year, we receive close to 2,700 letters
from high school football players who would like to know more about our
college football program. As you might imagine, all of the 2,700 football
players consider themselves to be pretty good in high school; otherwise,
they wouldn't be writing."

What about achievements such as All-League credentials? Says
Trainer: "While it's very nice for a youngster to have achieved those kinds
of awards in high school, as college football coaches, we really aren't that
impressed with those kinds of distinctions. First of all, it seems that every
kid has some sort of credential, and secondly, it's hard to gauge how a
youngster is selected for those kinds of awards. As a result, we're more
interested in seeing the game films and in seeing the youngster in person."

In short, if your child has their heart set on playing in a Division I,
I-AA, or II program, their letter-writing campaign may not be all that
useful. However, for certain Division III programs, especially those
colleges with relatively smaller enrollments, such a letter might be
extremely helpful as those athletic programs may not receive the large
volume of mail as larger schools do. In this case, the coach is much more
likely to read your note, and follow up with a response.

As far as expecting your high school coach to help you in the college
recruiting process, many parents are surprised and flat-out disappointed
when they discover that their child's coach really hasn't done much to
"get the word out" to college coaches. But what parents do not understand
is that most high school coaches just don't have enough time in their busy
days to make phone calls or write letters about the seniors on their team.
Furthermore, in many cases, the high school coach really doesn't have
any network of college contacts to call upon. It's almost as though the high
school coaches know their world of other high school coaches well, and

the college coaches are in a parallel universe, where most of their contacts are other college coaches. But as far as high school coaches and college coaches having a complete network of each other goes, that really is a general misconception.

What might happen occasionally is that a college coach will contact a high school coach about a superstar player. This does happen, but it's almost only in the case where the athlete is one of those very rare individuals. For example, the player is a 7-footer in basketball, or a 300-lb. lineman in football, or a softball pitcher who throws serious gas. For the other 99% of high school athletes, the scenario is almost nonexistent where a college coach picks up the phone and asks a high school coach if he or she has any good players to recommend.

Sometimes, a junior or senior in high school will receive junk mail or email from a variety of college recruiting services. Please note that these services, if you seek to employ them, are paid for by you—not by the colleges. (This point is significant in that it contrasts other college recruiting services, which are subscribed to by colleges and are paid for by colleges. As you might imagine, the best possible scenario would be for your child to be on the college of your choice's subscription service. But that's something neither you or your child can control.)

The college recruiting service that you choose to pay for will cost anywhere from a few hundred dollars to as much as a thousand or more. Upon procuring the service, usually your student-athlete is asked to fill out a detailed questionnaire about their sports and academic careers; sometimes, you are asked for a photo or even some videotape. Once all of this is completed, the recruiting service then takes all the data and mails it out to hundreds of colleges.

Usually, within a few weeks, if the recruiting service is legitimate, your son or daughter will start to receive lots of mail and even some phone calls from college athletic programs. While this is a wonderful experience for your child—to run to the mailbox and receive a letter from a coach—please try to keep it in perspective, and to encourage your kid to do the same. For the most part, the letters will simply be form letters that are hand-stamped by the coach. College coaches send out thousands of these letters in the hope of occasionally finding a diamond in the rough.

But for the most part, the form letters are just that—form letters and nothing more. Please don't be deceived into thinking your student-athlete is a "recruit" just because of these letters—letters that were generated by the recruiting service that tipped off the college that your son or daughter may be interested in applying there.

How do you know if your child is a **real** recruit? Easy. Your student-athlete will start receiving letters from coaches, but these letters will be handwritten and personalized to your youngster. Or the coaches will call your son or daughter at home. Or they'll invite your child to come to the campus for an official visit to the school. In short, once you start getting truly personalized and individualized attention from a college coach, then you know your child is a real recruit.

Walk-Ons, Recruited Walk-Ons, and Scholarship Players

But what if your child is a top athlete and no one comes calling? Can't he or she be a "walk-on" and get a fair shot to make a college team as a "walk-on?"

First off, let's define our terms. A true "walk-on" athlete is a college student who was never formally recruited by the college coach. That means that when the youngster shows up on the first day for practice, the coach usually has no idea of who the student is, or where he's from, or what kind of athletic ability he or she has. The student is, quite literally, "walking on" the field of play and opting to try out for the team.

Then there is the "recruited walk-on" athlete. This is a youngster who the college coach does know something about, including the fact that the student is attending that college and plays that sport. (Most college coaches are able to access information from the admissions office regarding which of the recruited walk-on student-athletes have been accepted.) Unlike the traditional recruited athlete who is getting some form of athletic scholarship, the recruited walk-on is not getting any athletic money at all. In other words, the coach had to make a decision in the recruiting process, and the coach decided that Player A will be getting some scholarship dough, but Player B will not. That being said, the coach still would like Player B to attend the college and try out for the team. And in most cases, the smart coach will give the recruited walk-on as much opportunity to make the team as the recruited athlete.

Don't forget that officially recruited athletes—the ones who get a scholarship offer—are usually given more of a chance to make the team than walk-ons. Why? Because every coach has a boss (usually the athletic director) and common sense dictates that if there are more walk-ons starting ahead of the scholarship players on the team, the athletic director is going to call the coach on the carpet. "After all," the athletic director will say, "these scholarship kids are supposed to the best in the land. How come they've been beaten out by walk-ons?"

That's a tough—and potentially very embarrassing—question for a head college coach to be asked. And it's the major reason why scholarship kids always get second and third chances, whereas walk-ons don't.

Getting on the Coach's Radar Screen

Keep this reality in mind. **The vast majority of high school senior athletes are not recruited by colleges.** That doesn't mean that they aren't talented and dedicated athletes. It only means that, somehow, they either fell through the college recruiting cracks (of which there are plenty), or the athlete didn't do a good job of marketing themselves to college coaches, or perhaps they were injured in high school, or they went to a small school, or for that matter, they simply started growing late in their teenage years.

Whatever the reason, if your youngster is finishing their senior year in high school and really wants to try out for a college team in the fall, they still have a chance. Once they have their acceptance letter to the school of their choice, it's time to let the college coach know they're going to be there in the fall.

Let's work backwards. If you just show up for classes on the first day of the fall semester at State University, and suddenly decide to try out for a fall team, then you have really minimized your chances of making that team. First off, the coach will have no idea of who you are. Even if you get 10 minutes of their time, you have to go through a somewhat embarrassing recitation of your sports career ("Well, I played a lot of sports in high school, and my favorite sport was soccer. . ."). You get the idea. This is a very tough conversation to have, and often quite fruitless.

But, assuming the coach does allow you to try out, don't be surprised if it's a one-day tryout. That's because most college coaches know that the chances of finding a "diamond in the rough" with a true walk-on is so rare, that they don't want to waste much time conducting tryouts. Of course, if the coach does find someone who looks good, then that individual will be asked to stay on and practice with the other members of the team. But again, this is quite rare.

From the coach's perspective, their attitude might be: "Look, how dedicated can this youngster be about playing this sport in college if they didn't even have enough spark or enthusiasm to call me or contact me before they enrolled?" In truth, that's a good question. After all, the coach is looking only for serious athletes for his or her team.

Okay, let's move forward. If your son or daughter wants to try out for a sport in college, then as soon as they're accepted to that college they should write a letter to the coach that touts their athletic achievements and clearly states that they're eager to try out. This letter should also contain some letters of recommendation from the youngster's high school coach, high school athletic director, travel team coach, or other scouts.

Then, three or four weeks after the letter has been received by the college coach, the youngster should call the coach and ask about reporting dates in the fall, workout programs in the summer, and anything else they need to know about trying out. Even better, if the coach will be on campus over the summer, ask if your son or daughter can come by and meet them for a few minutes. Or, even better still, if you live near the college, perhaps the college coach can stop by during the summer and see you perform in a game or competition.

The point is—you need to get yourself on the coach's radar screen so that he or she at least knows your name, understands that you're a serious athlete, and is aware that you definitely want to be considered as a viable candidate in the fall. Does this mean that you'll make the team? Of course not. But it does at least get the coach to know you a little bit, and perhaps puts him of the mind that maybe you're one of those student-athletes who fell between the cracks.

What Are a Walk-On's Chances?

In truth, the chances of making a college team as a true walk-on are very slim. That's not just at the Division I level. It's just as difficult at Division II and even Division III as well. College coaches will gladly tell you that they spend as much as 60% of their time in recruiting future athletes. As such, they think they do a pretty good job of finding the right kids for their program. So you can see why they would give less credence to any walk-on athlete.

Besides, there are many college programs that don't even have try-outs at all. That situation might seem rather odd, and totally contrary to a college's belief in developing student-athletes. I recall speaking with the head baseball coach at a prestigious Ivy League school, and he flat out told me that "we don't have any kids trying out for the team during fall baseball." When I asked him whether that was odd, he simply said, "No—and the reason is because I don't allow kids to try out. Only the kids I recruit can be on the team."

As a former head baseball coach at a top-ranked Division II college, I must tell you that I thought this particular coach's philosophy was not only shortsighted, but also downright counterproductive. After all, when I ran my program, I let walk-ons work out for at least a few weeks before making any cuts; that is, I made very sure that I didn't overlook a kid who might be a real find for my program. And each year, I always found one or two ballplayers who, as walk-ons, made the team.

As a college coach and, more importantly, as an educator, I always felt I had a responsibility to allow a youngster to at least try out, and to do so for several sessions. Most college coaches find the process of cutting a kid to be quite painful; my attitude was that it was even more painful for the athlete than for the coach.

To sum up, if your youngster is a recruited athlete, then that's great. Enjoy the moment. But remember, that only happens to only a handful of high school seniors all over the country. Most kids can just hope that, as a walk-on, they'll make the college team. While it's fine to have that dream, make sure your athlete does a little self-marketing before arriving on campus.

Showcases, Camps, and Other Marketing Opportunities

One of the most pressing questions that will hang over your young athlete's head throughout his or her last year of high school is this: How will college coaches find me? After all, there are something like 20,000 high schools in the United States from which college coaches may recruit.

As mentioned earlier, most college coaches subscribe to a variety of college recruiting services that go out and find high school athletes. The "tip sheets" provided by these services help coaches at least find names of athletes, and usually offer the basic information regarding school, size, weight, handedness (right or left), grades, SAT and ACT scores, and so on.

The trick, of course, is for your son or daughter to somehow get their name on one of these recruit lists, but as you might imagine, that's not always very easy. It's not like you can merely call up a service, pay a fee, and have your athlete's name added. Rather, these lists are usually compiled by local contacts who spend hours going through a variety of sources to find promising high school athletes. These sources could be anything from newspaper accounts to word-of-mouth suggestions from high school coaches, refs, and umpires. Many times, these contacts scour the various travel teams in the area in search of the top athletes. But as good as these sources are, the best way to get on a college recruiter's list is to have your son or daughter take part in either a "showcase" or a "player camp event."

Showcases

Showcases are a relatively new phenomenon. They didn't even exist 15 or 20 years ago. Basically, showcases are a one- or two-day gathering where top youngsters come out and show their stuff. Let's take baseball to illustrate. A typical baseball showcase is held at either a local high school or college, usually on a weekend during the summer. Each youngster is routinely charged a fee (maybe $50 to $100) to participate. On the first day, basic drills are run (60-yard dash, batting practice, fielding practice, etc.). Depending on the number of kids in the showcase, this first day might last 3–4 hours. On the second day, the kids are usually divided into two teams, and a scrimmage game is played.

What makes the showcase extremely valuable is that college coaches from all over are invited to come and watch the participants. That's the key. For two days, your youngster can be seen—live and in person—by numerous college coaches. In baseball, there's a wonderful showcase called the "Top 96" which is held every summer in New England. As you might imagine, it's supposed to attract the top 96 players from the area, but in recent years, that number has grown a bit.

Each year, the Top 96 will attract as many as 80–90 college baseball coaches (Divisions I, II, and III) and perhaps 20 pro scouts. In other words, if your son is a serious baseball player *and* has some real skills, then a showcase like the Top 96 is the place to be seen. In addition, once he's been at this kind of showcase, his name immediately and automatically goes on the sort of recruit lists discussed above. It's as though he's now qualified to be a real recruit.

But there is one major caveat in all of this. Because showcases have become so popular in recent years, more and more entrepreneurs have seen these as real money-making opportunities and have started their own. As a consumer, you have to do a little homework first to make sure the showcase is going to be worth your kid's time and your money. The questions to ask include:

1. How long has this showcase been around? (If it's brand new or less than a few years old, be a little wary.)

2. How much does it cost? (Most of the more reliable showcases don't cost more than $75–$100.)

3. How many college coaches have already committed to be there? (If it's less than 20, again, be suspicious. And remember that new showcase operators will probably try to exaggerate the number of coaches.)

4. Most importantly, is this an "invitation-only" showcase, or is it open to anyone who comes by? (Obviously, if anyone who has some dough can sign up, right away you know that this is simply a money-making venture, and that the quality of athletic talent is not going to be that high.)

Player Camps

Camps are like showcases, except that they may last as long as a week or so, and are often held on a particular college campus. Let's use football as an example. Your son gets literature in the mail, or hears about a "camp for recruits" from his high school coach that's going to be held for a week at State University. The fee might run as much as $300–$500, and of course, in addition to seeing the college up close and in person, there's also the guarantee that he'll be seen by the head college coach and/or his staff.

So far, so good. But again, it pays to do some homework. These camps are, first and foremost, meant to be money-making ventures for the college and the football staff. Many times, they're open to anyone who wants to come, which is fine, except that the talent level may vary quite a bit. You should also know that it's the rare camp in which the head college coach actually comes to the field and spends a lot of quality time with the campers. In fact, many times the head coach might spend no more than an hour during the entire camp talking to the kids; the rest of the camp is run by his staff.

As a parent considering spending significant money on a camp, just be aware of the realities of this situation. If nothing else, your son will have an opportunity to see a college campus, meet some college coaches, and also meet other kids who aspire to play college ball. And if your son really stands out from the others, then his name will definitely start to pop up on college recruiting lists. But beyond that, be careful of your son's expectations, abilities, and desire when considering a player camp.

What about "P.G." (post-graduate) Programs?

If your son or daughter has been seemingly overlooked by college recruiters—whether they were injured in high school, or they were late bloomers, or they played for a small high school with a low profile, or simply because they got overlooked by all the college recruiters—then one option is to look into having your youngster attend a prep school for another year of schooling.

Traditionally, the decision to complete an extra year of high school at a prep school was usually made if a youngster wanted to attend an elite academic college but didn't have the requisite grades to be admitted. This "post-graduate" year of high school, also known as a "P.G." year, allowed the youngster to apply himself or herself more in the classroom, get a better grade-point average, and then apply to the colleges of their choice with a better chance of becoming accepted. P.G. years of study are available to all kinds of students, but for student-athletes, that extra year of study allows them to not only get better grades, but also add another year of muscle, weight, and experience to their athletic skills.

P.G. study programs have long been popular options for promising football and ice hockey players, but over the last decade, they have also become useful to athletes in other sports, such as basketball. And it helps to know that college recruiters always check out the athletic talent at the better-known prep schools around the country.

As a result, if you feel that your son or daughter could really benefit from that extra year of study, maturity, and athletic development, ask your school's guidance counselor for more information. And, ask your high school or travel team coach as well. Prep schools, especially boarding schools, can be very, very expensive, running as much as $25,000 per year. But most of these schools offer lots of scholarship money as well.

The key, however, is to do your homework early on. If you wait until after your son or daughter has already graduated from high school, then it may be too late to get him or her accepted into a prep school. As a precaution, if it seems by the fall of their senior year that not much is happening in terms of college coaches knocking down your door, then that's the time to start looking into prep schools. Like most colleges, these prep schools will have your son or daughter go through a regular admissions process. And odds are that those who apply earliest have the most chance of being accepted.

IT'S NEVER TOO EARLY!

Most sports parents understandably assume that college coaches will start writing letters and making calls when their son or daughter is going into their senior year. But that thinking is wrong.

Most top-flight college coaches will actually start looking for talented kids to help their program when the student is in 9th, 10th, or 11th grade. These coaches know that the sooner they can pinpoint a prospect, the sooner they can start to try and sway that youngster to go to their college. If the coach waits until the kid is a senior, he and his program will have a lot of catching up to do with other college coaches.

As such, it's a good idea to have your 9th or 10th grader get as much exposure as possible. Showcases, summer camps, player camps, travel programs—you name it. The more your kid's name is known to the coaches in these circles, the more chance your child has of getting their name onto one of the coaches' recruit lists.

CHAPTER NINE:
The Mental Side of Sports and Performance Enhancement

Back when I was playing college and then professional baseball in the early and mid-1970s, I kept hearing tantalizing rumors that certain elite athletes, most notably Olympians, were using all sorts of radical psychological training to make themselves into better performers. Terms like "pre-set routines" and "self-hypnotherapy" and "visualization" had been literally unheard of up until those days, and yet I kept reading magazine articles in which these terms were being introduced.

At the time, this new dimension of training (now known as sports psychology, or performance-enhancement training) was really being administered at a grassroots level. Even if mainstream coaches and athletes had heard of this kind of advanced mental training, it was routinely either poked fun at or denigrated. I can still recall one of my professional coaches scoffing at the new training, and summing it all up with a perfect Yogi-ism: "Any ballplayer who needs to see a sports shrink ought to have his head examined!"

But despite the initial reluctance from the old guard, the younger athletes—especially those who were eager to find any edge they could to improve their game—started to explore and learn more about these novel techniques. I can still recall being a sophomore in college and reading a fascinating book called *Psycho-Cybernetics* by a surgeon named Dr. Maxwell Maltz. In short, Dr. Maltz proposed that one should indeed have total control over one's muscles if one wanted to perform at a peak level. And to reach this level of total control, one merely had to see one performing well in their mind's eye, over and over. In effect, the more you pictured yourself performing a difficult task in a thoroughly competent way, the more you "trained" your neuromuscular system to expect to perform well.

This is the basis of *visualization*, which is known these days to every coach at the high school and college and pro levels. But in the early 1970s, Dr. Maltz's approach to mentally training oneself to perform at a peak level was groundbreaking. As I recall, he used this system to prepare himself to be a topflight surgeon. To accomplish this, he would prepare for a delicate surgical procedure by visualizing exactly each step of the operation. By "seeing" the procedure slowly, clearly, and successfully, he was "training" himself to be prepared for the actual operation. In effect, when he walked into the operating room the next day, because he had so thoroughly rehearsed himself through visualization, the operation would feel as though it was a routine procedure. After all, in his mind's eye, Dr. Maltz had already successfully performed this operation many, many times.

Applying Visualization to Sports

The very same principle that Dr. Maltz followed is now used in sports. Athletes are usually asked to lie down on a bed during the day for 20 minutes. The room should be dark and quiet—no background music, or any other distractions at all. The athlete should then stretch out, relax by taking some deep breaths, and let all of the stress from the day leave their body.

With eyes closed, the athlete then begins a sequence in which they see their next game or competition or performance in vivid detail in their mind. These visualized scenes should be played out in detail and in color. One should truly *see* oneself getting ready to compete. Most importantly, as the critical moments of their performance are played out in the mind's eye, the athlete must see himself or herself throwing that perfect curve ball, or executing a perfect gymnastics routine, or hitting a key free throw with no time left on the clock. In short, the athlete must constantly see himself or herself performing brilliantly, over and over again. Again, repetition is the key to making this happen.

The theory behind visualization is that the body will respond to this kind of constant positive reinforcement, and that the brain can truly "pretrain" the muscles of the body to always respond in just the right sequence so that peak performances are guaranteed. After all, every top athlete, whether they're swinging a golf club or a tennis racquet or a baseball bat, is always looking for total consistency in their performance. Visualization techniques can—and do—provide exactly that kind of training.

Does it work? For the most part, I believe it does, although the results will depend on the individual athlete. Will it work for your young athlete? I can't answer that question. But I will say this: if nothing else, if your athlete faithfully uses visualization techniques as part of their training, eventually the process will become a powerful part of their preparation for any kind of competition. And that alone will build a sense of self-esteem and self-confidence which they can tap into to handle any kind of difficult situation.

Introducing Mental Cue Cards

There are, of course, other methods to help a young athlete step up their mental preparation for any performance. One of my favorite techniques **for maintaining a certain level of consistency** is utilizing something I call the **"Mental Cue Card."**

The Mental Cue Card is a simple yet very powerful technique. When an athlete is at a level where he or she is doing well in their performances,

I ask them right after a game to take an index card and then to write down as precisely as possible the five or six personalized keys they noticed when they were performing. This list should be written down right away, and again, the more detailed and personalized the better.

For example: A golfer, who has been having some trouble with his putting, comes off a wonderful day on the golf course when everything seemed to work well for him. As a result, his mental cue card—written just after his performance—might read like this:

- Always take two deep breaths before I start to line up the putt.
- Crouch down behind the ball. First, look at the ball. Then, look at the hole.
- Grip the putter and waggle it three times to keep my hands loose.
- See the hole and see the ball again. Focus only on the hole—reduce all other distractions.
- Let my hands become part of the club.
- Trust my athletic instincts.

Understand that the mental cue card should be unique to every athlete. You're merely trying to precisely pinpoint how you feel and to record the special, personalized things you do before you execute—in this case—a perfect putt.

Then, to maximize the impact of your mental cue card, you should always carry it with you so that you never forget what works for you, and what doesn't. **More importantly, refer to it often and read it slowly and completely before every competition.** That's essential. You never want to be in a situation where you didn't perform or play well because you forgot to consult your mental cue card before the game. This review should become part of your pre-game ritual.

Give it a try. If nothing else, the sooner you memorize every aspect of your mental cue card, the closer you'll be to maximizing your performance on a consistent basis.

Getting In "The Zone"

The Zone. It's where every athlete wants to be. It's a psychological state in which the athlete is so focused on what he or she is doing, that everything around them is no longer a distraction. Some athletes describe the sensation as experiencing the game action suddenly slowing down to the point where they can easily throw a curve ball for a strike, or throw a perfect touchdown pass, or hit winner after winner on the tennis court.

This phenomenon is also known as "a state of flow." In this state, the athlete is so consumed by the competition at hand that their other senses are seemingly shut down so that they can totally be in tune with their desire to play well. Here's how one high school basketball player described being "in the zone" or in "a state of flow" when he caught fire and rattled off 22 points in the second half of a game in which he scored just 6 points in the first half:

"I was playing okay during the first half of the basketball game. Nothing special, just okay. Some of my shots went in and some didn't. But somehow, after halftime, everything just seemed to click. . . . I hit my first shot, then my second shot, and then another, and before I knew it, whatever kind of shot I put up the ball went in.

"It seemed like everything was in slow motion. And the basketball hoop was gigantic—like I couldn't miss. I guess I sensed the fans in the stands were cheering for me during the second half, but honestly I never heard them. I just kept firing away, and the ball kept going in, again and again. It was like I was in a perfect state of mind. And before I knew it, the game was over. The time just flew by."

All of these experiences are typical of being in the zone: totally focused, all the action seems to slow down around you, there's a lack of awareness of outside distractions, and curiously, the time seems to go by quickly. Most of all, there's that wonderful feeling of being in a perfect state of mind, where everything seems so easy, so effortless.

As you might imagine, all top athletes want to be in the zone when they compete. And many of them do, in fact, get there more often than you might think. Problem is, no sports psychologist or performance enhancement coach has found a surefire way or method yet to deliver "the zone" to an athlete on a consistent basis. Of course, if such a way were discovered, athletes would flock to it immediately. But it hasn't happened yet.

Pre-Set Ritual or Simple Superstition?

So what do athletes do to find the right focus? Like the medieval alchemists who tried desperately to find a formula to make gold from ordinary substances, athletes today will often review what pre-game activities they carried out before they played well in a particular game. Their sense is that perhaps they can effectively replicate their zone if only they could pinpoint a precise pre-game ritual, or meal, or routine that worked for them in the past.

As a result, most athletes do, in fact, have pre-set, pre-game rituals. Ironically, some of these rituals are interpreted—especially by the fans—as being simply superstitious. Actually, the athletes are not really being "superstitious." They're simply trying to find that comfort area that may launch them into the zone. For example, the great baseball hitter Wade Boggs was known only to eat chicken dishes on game day. Superstition? No, it was just his way of trying to get himself and his body ready to play in the zone. Nomar Garciapparra, the great shortstop for the Boston Red Sox, also goes through an elaborate ritual before each pitch: he checks his batting helment, tugs on his batting gloves, kicks the dirt from his shoes, and so on. Superstition? No, it's just his way of trying to get himself into the zone.

Other players, of course, have their own ways of getting ready to perform at peak level. Perhaps it's the way they wear their uniform, or tie their shoes, or select a certain type of chewing gum. Whatever that pre-game ritual may be, it may appear to an outsider to be a silly superstition—but it's not a superstition at all.

How can you explain these techniques to your youngster? First, start with the basics. Let them know that they might want to think about developing their own pre-game ritual or routine that they can utilize before they perform. Most little kids won't take this seriously, but as kids get a little older (around 12 or 13), they'll find their own routine that works for them. Remind them, as they develop this routine, that it should become part of every performance they go through.

And what about actual superstitions? Should you actively discourage your child from developing these kinds of notions? From my experience—whether the kid likes to wear the same smelly game socks each week or eat breakfast off the same plate every game day—the vast majority of superstitions are fine. A superstition should only be discouraged if it is potentially dangerous to the young athlete or to their teammates or opponents. The other concern with superstitions is whether they become too time-consuming for the athlete to follow.

Most importantly, if the young athlete does happen to have a good game on a day in which the superstitions were not followed, then it's not a bad idea to point out that the superstitious pre-game routine obviously did not have any impact on their performance. In other words, at some point you want to stress to your athlete that it's really their athletic talent and hard work that propels them to top performances—not their superstitions.

What's the Right Age to Begin Performance Enhancement?

From my experience, trying to introduce young kids (under the age of 12) to sports psychology and performance enhancement techniques really doesn't work very well. Kids at those tender ages are still more focused—

and rightfully so—on just having fun in their sports than worrying about achieving peak performance. In fact, it's also been my experience that kids don't start taking performance enhancement seriously until their late teens.

But once the youngster starts becoming more focused on their sport, that's the time to introduce them to the practice of visualization. And, of course, videotape training (see box below) is essential through these years as well. The more in tune the athlete is with their head and their body's actions, the more proficient they're going to become. Even better, they'll become more self-confident as well. **And a heightened sense of self-confidence always produces better performances and better results.**

Let's take a minute to put a chronology on all of this. First, let the kids play sports for the pure fun of it all when they're ages 5–13. They may develop some of their own superstitions during this time, but that's okay. Just remind them that superstitions will only carry them so far; it's really practice and more practice that will take them to where they want to go.

When they reach the middle school years (13–14), you can at least introduce the concept of sports psychology to the athlete. But again, don't expect the youngster to do much here except try to understand that performance enhancement techniques do exist. Very few athletes this young will put any of the techniques into practice.

It's during their high school years that serious athletes will start thinking more and more about somehow gaining that extra edge on their opponents, or that they want to become more consistent in their performances. By this age they can start to train with visualization techniques, or develop their own mental cue cards, and of course, start to develop a pre-game ritual. Ultimately, they will become familiar with these techniques, and by the time they start college they will have developed their own style and approach.

Videotaping Your Athlete as an Instructional Tool

These days, it seems that every parent who has a child playing a sport always brings a video camera to record the kid's performance in the games. That's fine; if nothing else, the videotape serves as a keepsake for the youngster to look at when they get older. The video serves as a kind of modern-day "scrapbook" for the young athlete.

But what's always been curious to me about all those parents who videotape their kids is that I'm not sure they realize how that video can really aid their kids in terms of actual instruction and in improving their play. That is, if you take the time and learn the best ways to videotape some of your child's performances, **then you can have the tape serve two purposes: one, as a family scrapbook that the youngster can watch over and over again for fun or for memories; and two, as a truly invaluable instructional tool.**

For well over thirty years, sports psychologists have urged serious athletes to learn how to "visualize" their performances in upcoming games. As discussed earlier, the process of visualization works on the theory that your brain subconsciously controls your body's neuromuscular system, and if you can "pre-program" your key neuromuscular connections to perform in just the right way, then you can, in effect, program your athletic body to always perform at a high level.

Visualization techniques have been used around the world, and for the most part, top athletes find that this approach works for them, although in varying degrees. But more recently, in a study reported in the Association for the Advancement of Applied Sports Psychology, it was discovered that top athletes can also benefit greatly from watching videotaped performances of themselves in action. This video instruction works very well when athletes have a chance to observe themselves performing at an optimum level. Indeed, many top sports psychologists (myself included) suggest that struggling athletes watch video "highlight" reels of themselves over and over again, so that the visual imagery sinks in. The key in this process is that the videotape should show those plays where the athlete performed well (e.g. making all of their shots from the court, having a perfect drive off the tee, etc.). By watching videotape of top performances, an athlete can begin to find that "groove" that they're looking for.

Pro and college athletes will often spend several hours in the videotape room, first looking at one of their poor performances, and then contrasting that tape with their personal highlight reel. Invariably, the athlete will find some key difference in their technique or approach that made a big difference in their performances. This difference may be very subtle to the outsider, but it'll be very apparent to the individual athlete who can compare their own styles from both tapes.

So How Do I Perform "Video Visualization?"

There are some basic steps to follow. First, of course, be very familiar with the videotaping camera. Get a handle on how to zoom in for close action. Realize that if you have to shoot directly into the sunlight, chances are you won't get much clear action on the tape. Naturally, your best bet is to shoot the action with the sun at your back.

Then there's the problem of trying to find the right spot on the field to tape your child. If your son or daughter is playing on a field which is surrounded by a chain link fence, you'll have to experiment as to what's the best way to shoot either through, or over, the mesh of the fence. Scout out the surroundings before play gets underway so that you find the optimum videotaping location.

If the weather is very cold or wet, you'll have other problems. You have to make certain that the lens does not get wet, or even covered with light condensation. Be prepared to bring along whatever essentials you need to make sure you're ready to take care of the videotaping process. Naturally, a lot of this is common sense. But to do the job right, it takes some planning—and some experimenting—to make certain you know the best way to tape the games in order to catch your son or daughter in action.

The sport your kid plays will determine how difficult it is, or isn't, to get some quality footage of them in action. Baseball and softball, of course, are relatively simple. Videotaping a pitcher from behind the backstop, or shooting tape of a hitter from the side of the backstop, is easy. But trying to tape a youngster playing in a soccer game or field hockey game is most challenging because, quite frankly, you never know when the ball is going to his or her part of the field. You have to learn how to anticipate when the action is going to involve your child, and then be ready to start recording before it actually does.

Then—and most importantly—you have to discipline yourself not to jostle the camera when you're taping the action. This, of course, tends to be somewhat nerve-wracking as it is difficult to stay focused on taping when everybody around you is cheering. Also, when you're taping, you're not really watching the game like a normal spectator. Many times when I have taped my children playing sports—that is, looking almost nonstop through a small eyepiece on the camera—I really didn't get a chance to see and enjoy the action while it was actually happening. I had to wait to watch the videotape later in the day; but when I did, I was able to sit down and share the joy with my kids.

When Your Youngster Views the Tape

As a sports parent, this is where you have to be a little patient. When your child first sits down to watch the videotape, allow them the pleasure of watching the tape several times straight through and without much discussion. With the first few times they watch it, realize that they're going to watch the tape as they would watch a movie or television show. That is, they're watching simply for fun and for pleasure—not so much to analyze their actions.

But once they have enjoyed the tape a few times, then you might want to invite them—and this is strictly an invite, never a demand—to sit down and go over their individual plays together. Just as a football coach will watch videotape of previous games to gain knowledge, you can go over the various highlights of your child's performance. Note: to keep your youngster absorbed, go over the high points of their performance first. Heap lots of praise on them for the plays in which they did well.

Note again: this is not the time to focus on those parts of their game where they made mistakes and played poorly. Remember: the purpose of the videotape session is to recognize and reinforce those positive parts of their game. The idea here is to take visualization to a higher level in their mind's eye. That is, if they can literally see themselves doing well on the video—and they can watch the video over and over again—then they are, in effect, programming their mind, muscles, and nervous system to be consistent in their most outstanding athletic actions.

It will come as no surprise that professional baseball players are huge devotees of this form of video visualization. They will, in effect, look at highlight reels of themselves hitting well or pitching well. The same technique is used by professional and collegiate basketball players who want to see and study their form in shooting a jump shot or a free throw. In fact, this technique is commonly used by just about all professional athletes in all sports these days—that is, those athletes who want to reinforce consistent athletic patterns in their performances.

Coaches, instructors, and athletes have all found that there's no better way to communicate technique improvements than by having the athlete view himself or herself on tape. Most parents take video of their kids' games and then put the tapes away in some sort of video scrapbook. But there's nothing at all wrong with letting your child become familiar and comfortable with the use of videotape to see how they can strengthen and improve their game.

IN CONCLUSION. . . .

I wrote at the beginning of this book that, as the parent of a budding athlete, you have to first figure out what's the ultimate goal for your son or daughter in sports. If the overall goal is to watch your athlete develop into a professional or collegiate player, you have to understand that that goal is very ambitious. And a cursory look at the odds would convince just about anyone that banking on a pro career is ill-advised. Of course, I did not promise that this book would help any athlete reach the big-time.

But what I did promise was that this book would provide a general overview of how you could help your child reach their God-given potential in sports—in terms of both developing skills and having fun. To me, that has always been my overall goal for my own children, and from my experience, that's been the best way to approach sports.

Let's never forget that playing sports is still—at the very core—based upon having fun. That's why our kids (and ourselves) are attracted to competitive athletics in the first place. It's fun for us to see how our skills and talents stack up against our friends. Indeed, that's where our children get their first taste of competition, usually when they are merely 5 or 6 years old. And if they find that they enjoyed the experience of competition, then they usually want to come back and play some more. From those very modest games, their ambitions, dreams, and hopes begin to build and grow.

That's the inherent attraction of playing sports. Building—and chasing—dreams is what life is all about for kids. And as caring parents, who want only the best for our children, our job is to be supportive in their quest to pursue their dreams. Our young children don't come into sports knowing about failure or rejection or adversity; but alas, as grown-ups we do know about these things. That's why it's so important that we're there to help them when they stumble and fall. And in my experience, I have yet to meet an athlete—even the most accomplished—who didn't occasionally have to deal with adversity.

So, after their last game, if you can still reach out and hug your child, and find a smile on their face, then you know that you've done your job well as their parent. Ultimately, at some point in every athlete's career, the question must be faced of just how far they can, or want, to go with their sporting career. We know, statistically, that for more than 95% of all high school athletes, their organized sports career ends with that last varsity game. A few lucky ones go on and play in college or maybe even in the pros. But even for those lucky few, they're just pushing back the clock a couple of years more. Eventually, all athletes—even the great ones—have to "hang 'em up" and retire as an active participant.

The Sports Parents' Final Questionnaire

So how does a parent know if he or she has done a good job in raising their athlete? Is it all about whether the youngster has become a star player—or does it matter more that the child simply enjoyed playing the game? To me, when it's all said and done, the major questions every parent should be able to ask their athletic child are:

Was it fun?

Did you have a good time?

Did you work hard at your sport?

Were you respected by your teammates?

What were your all-time favorite moments that you'll never forget?

Did you give it all you had?

Do you have wonderful memories that will last you a lifetime?

And finally, did I make it fun for you?

APPENDIX A:
Selected Books on Sports and Sports Parenting

Each year it seems that dozens of new books on sports parenting techniques are published. Yet from my perspective, only a few really stand out from all the rest. Here's a selective bibliography of what I have found to be the top books (and other sources) on sports and sports parenting.

Bigelow, Bob, and Tom Moroney and Linda Hall, *Just Let the Kids Play* (Health Communications, Inc.: 2001).

Bird, Larry, *Bird Watching: On Playing and Coaching the Game I Love* (Warner Books: 1999). On August 18, 1992, Larry Bird announced his retirement from the Boston Celtics. He says, "It was one of the happiest days of [my] life." Just as he stunned opponents with over-the-shoulder passes, killer steals, and jaw-dropping long-range jumpers on the court, Larry Bird offers one startling revelation after another.

Bissinger, H.G., and Rob Clark, Jr., *Friday Night Lights: A Town, A Team, and a Dream* (Da Capo Press: 2000). Secular religions are fascinating in the devotion and zealousness they breed, and in Texas, high school football has its own rabid hold over the faithful. H.G. Bissinger, a Pulitzer Prize-winning journalist, enters into the spirit of one of its most fervent shrines: Odessa, Texas.

Blais, Madeleine, *In These Girls, Hope is a Muscle: A True Story of Hoop Dreams and One Very Special Team* (Warner Books: 1995). They were a talented team with a near-perfect record. But for five straight years, when it came to the crunch of the playoffs, the Amherst Lady Hurricanes—a "finesse" high school girls' basketball team of nice girls from a nice town—somehow lacked the scrappy, hard-driving desire to win the big game.

Bradley, Bill. *Values of the Game* (Bantam Doubleday Dell Publishing: 2000). Bill Bradley, U.S. Senator from New Jersey from 1979 to 1997 and a member of two championship New York Knicks teams, returns to the scene of his first career, and his first great passion, basketball.

Bredemeier, Brenda, *Character Development and Physical Activity* (Human Kinetics Publishing: 1995).

Burnett, Ph.D., Darrell J., *It's Just a Game* (iUniverse.com: 2001). In place of a third printing of his original book, *Youth, Sports, & Self-Esteem: A Guide for Parents*, Dr. Darrell Burnett, a published authority on parenting, decided to revise his popular book, adding some sportsmanship check lists, and changing the title to *It's Just a Game!*

Bylsma, Dan and Jay M., *So You Want to Play in the NHL: A Guide for Young Players* (Contemporary Books: 2001). So you want to play in the NHL? Prepare for life. Starting in the family backyard ice rink, Dan Bylsma realized his dream of playing in the NHL. But how he got there might surprise you.

Bylsma, Dan and Jay M., *So Your Son Wants to Play in the NHL* (Sleeping Bear Press: 1998). It is midnight in Grand Haven, Michigan. Floodlights and shouts fill the air as the Bylsma boys skate wildly around the only ice rink in the city. Nobody can shoo them home, because they are home. The rink is in their backyard.

Clark, Bobby, *Coaching Youth Soccer: A Baffled Parent's Guide* (McGraw Hill Professional Publishing: 1999). "Coaching is simply another word for teaching."—Bobby Clark

Coleman, Ellen, R.D., M.A., M.P.H. *The Ultimate Sports Nutrition Handbook* (Bull Publishing: 1996). *The Ultimate Sports Nutrition Handbook* provides proven strategies that athletes can use to perform closer to their potential. It presents current information that athletes from the weekender to the professional, school-ager to senior—can put to use immediately to enjoy better performance and overall health.

Csikszentmihalhyi, Mihaly, *Flow: The Psychology of Optimal Experience.* You have heard about how a musician loses herself in her music, how a painter becomes one with the process of painting. In work, sport, conversation or hobby, you have experienced, yourself, the suspension of time, the freedom of complete absorption in activity. This is "flow."

Damon, William, *Greater Expectations: Overcoming the Culture of Indulgence in Our Homes and Schools. Greater Expectations* is the book that exposed the low standards that children are confronted with in our homes, our schools, and throughout our culture. It exploded many of the misconceptions about children and how to raise them, including the cult of self-esteem, "child-centered" learning, and other overly indulgent practices.

Dorrance, Anson. *Training Soccer Champions* (JTC Sports, Inc.: 1996). *Training Soccer Champions* gives insight into the theories, philosophies and methods used by Dorrance to become one of the most effective and successful soccer coaches in the world.

Doyle, Jr., Daniel E., *Are You Watching, Adolph Rupp?* (Stadia Publishing, 1989). There exists today a sinister element in sports where the love of money, success, and fame grows uncontrolled. Unfortunately, many leaders are more concerned with victories, fundraising, and personal gain than they are with developing positive character traits and physical well-being.

Engh, Fred. *Why Johnny Hates Sports* (Square One Publishers: 2002). "Mom, do I really have to go the game? Can't I just stay home?" All across the country, an ever-increasing amount of children are dropping out of organized sports—in soccer, baseball, football, swimming and more.

Faber, Adele, Elaine Mazlish and Kimberly Ann Coe, *How to Talk So Kids Listen and Listen So Kids Will Talk* (Avon Books: 1999). *How to Talk So Kids Will Listen and Listen So Kids Will Talk* is an excellent communication tool based on a series of workshops developed by

Adele Faber and Elaine Mazlish. Faber and Mazlish (co-authors of *Siblings Without Rivalry*) provide a step-by-step approach to improving relationships in your house.

Grace & Glory: A Century of Women in the Olympics (Multi-Media Partners Ltd. and Triumph Books: 1996). At the first modern-day Olympic Games in Athens in 1896, women were barred from competing, but a young woman named Melpomene unofficially ran the marathon event, despite widespread belief that women were incapable of such a feat.

Gregg, Lauren with Tim Nash, *The Champion Within: Training for Excellence* (JTC Sports: 1999). In my career as a player and as a coach, I have had the privilege of being at the forefront of the growth of the women's game.

Isenberg, Marc. *The Student-Athlete Survival Guide* (Ragged Mountain Press/McGraw Hill: 2001). *The Student-Athlete Survival Guide* is the resource for high school and college athletes, their parents, and coaches.

Jackson, Phil and Hugh Delehanty, *Sacred Hoops: Spiritual Lessons of a Hardwood Warrior* (Hyperion:1996). *Sacred Hoops* is an inside look at the higher wisdom of teamwork from former Chicago Bulls' head coach, Phil Jackson. At the heart of the book is Jackson's philosophy of mindful basketball—and his lifelong quest to bring enlightenment to the competitive world of professional sports.

Jackson, Phil, and Charley Rosen, *More Than a Game* (Seven Stories Press: 2001). The parallel lives of the reigning NBA champion coach and basketball's "foremost literary chronicler" (with the *Wall Street Journal*), serve here as the jumping off point for an exploration into the deeper truths that abound in the game of basketball.

Jackson, Susan A., and Mihaly Csikszentmihalyi, *Flow in Sports* (Human Kinetics Publishing: 1999). The experience of flow is still one of the least understood phenomena in sport. And yet it is one of the richest, most memorable experiences an athlete will ever know. Some call it a natural "high." Others refer to it as being "in the zone."

Janda, MD, David, *The Awakening of a Surgeon* (Sleeping Bear Press, 2001). *The Awakening of a Surgeon* is the incredible story of his passion to make the lives of athletes of all ages safer. *The Awakening of a Surgeon* is a great book about making sports safer for your kids.

Janssen, M.S., Jeff, *Championship Team Building: What Every Coach Needs to Know to Build a Motivated, Committed & Cohesive Team* (Winning the Mental Game: 1999). Learn the Secret Formulas for Creating Team Chemistry. Written specifically for coaches, this groundbreaking book details dozens of proven strategies for building a championship team in any sport at any level.

Kindlon, Ph.D., Dan, *Raising Cain* (Ballantine Books: 2000). Dan Kindlon, Ph.D. and Michael Thompson, Ph.D., two of the country's leading child psychologists, share what they have learned in more than thirty-five years of combined experience working with boys and their families.

Kuchenbecker, Ph.D., Shari, *Raising Winners: A Parent's Guide to Helping Kids Succeed* (Times Books: 2000). Whether your child is a casual joiner or a serious athlete, the playing field is a terrific place to learn confidence, sportsmanship, and other skills he or she will need to succeed in life.

Leonard, George, *Mastery: The Keys to Success and Long-term Fulfillment* (Plume Publishing: 1992). Drawing on Zen philosophy and his expertise in the martial art of aikido, bestselling author George Leonard shows how the process of mastery can help us attain a higher level of excellence and a deeper sense of satisfaction and fulfillment in our daily lives.

Loehr, Ed.D., James E., *Mental Toughness Training for Sports: Achieving Athletic Excellence* (Penguin Books, 1982). Is your game not quite as good as it should be? Do you train hard, only to find that at critical moments your concentration—not your skill—fails you? Winning athletes possess more than physical prowess. They are mentally tough.

Maraniss, David. *When Pride Still Mattered* (Touchstone Books: 2000). *When Pride Still Mattered* is the quintessential story of the American family: how Vince Lombardi, the son of an immigrant Italian butcher, rose to the top, and how his character and will to prevail transformed him, his wife, his children, his players, his sport, and ultimately the entire country.

Margolis, Jeffrey. *Violence in Sports: Victory at What Price?* (Enslow Publishers Inc.: 1999). Fierce financial competition among team owners and corporate sponsors, the determination of players to win, and the fanaticism of fans have all played a part in the rise of sports violence.

McIntosh, Peter, *Fair Play: Ethics in Sport and Education* (Heinemann: 1979). Does fair play have a future? We know it has a past because that is where the words and ideas came from. But how real is fair play; how much is it a myth?

McPhee, John, *A Sense of Where You Are* (Farrar Straus & Giroux: 1999). First published in 1965, *A Sense of Where You Are* is the literary equivalent of a harmonic convergence, a remarkable confluence of two talents—John McPhee and Bill Bradley—at the beginning of what would prove to be long and distinguished careers.

Metzl, Dr. Jordan, *The Young Athlete: A Sport Doctor's Complete Guide for Parents* (Little Brown & Company: 2002).

Murphy, Austin. *The Sweet Season: A Sportswriter Rediscovers Football, Family, and a Bit of Faith at Minnesota's St. John's University* (HarperCollins: 2001). Looking to escape the NFL for a while, sports journalist Austin Murphy spends a sabbatical at St. John's College, a small Benedictine School in rural Minnesota, with the best record in college football history.

Newby-Fraser, Paula, and John M. Mora, *Peak Fitness for Women* (Human Kinetics: 1995). Go beyond the basics of training with Paula Newby Fraser's *Peak Fitness for Women!* In this book, seven-time Hawaii Ironman champion Paula Newby-Fraser presents a total fitness program that shows you how to overcome personal barriers and realize your athletic potential in training and competition.

Pipher, Dr. Mary, *Reviving Ophelia: Saving the Selves of Adolescent Girls* (Ballantine Books: 1995). Why are more American adolescent girls prey to depression, eating disorders, addictions, and suicide attempts than ever before? According to Dr. Mary Pipher, a clinical psychologist who has treated girls for more than twenty years, we live in a look-obsessed, media-saturated, "girl-poisoning" culture.

Pollack, Dr. William, *Real Boys: Rescuing Our Boys from the Myths of Manhood.*

Rhoads, Rick. *The Money Sucker Machine: The Truth About Gambling and How It Destroys Lives* (2001). This booklet shows why gambling is a loser's game. Read it and inoculate yourself against the gambling epidemic that is sweeping across high school and college campuses. "Everyone bets?" Not if you don't.

Riley, Pat, *The Winner Within: A Life Plan for Team Players* (Berkeley Books: 1993). He's one of America's greatest coaches, known for inspiring the champions of pro basketball to work as a team—in short, Pat Riley is the master of creating success.

Sanders, Summer, *Champions are Raised, Not Born: How My Parents Made Me a Success* (Dell Books: 2000). "What's the measure of your success as a parent? A kid who beats all the pros before he's a teenager? Who's worth a billion dollars before he's thirty? I'm writing this book to suggest a different standard, a better measure of successful parenting."

Scott, Nina Savin, *Smart Soccer: How to Use Your Mind to Play Your Best* (The Millbrook Press: 1999). Negative thoughts, distractions, pressure from parents, dwelling on mistakes—these are just a few of the problems that may get in the way of a young soccer player's performance.

Selleck, Ph.D., George, and Davind Canning Epperson, Ph.D., *Beyond the Bleachers: The Art of Parenting Today's Athletes* (Alliance Publishers, 2000). In today's world, parents must look long and hard to find positive influences for their children. Sports provide parents with the ideal laboratory for teaching life's lessons and making a real difference in their children's lives.

Selleck, Ph.D., George, and David Canning Epperson, Ph.D., *From the Bleachers with Love: Advice to Parents with Kids in Sports* (Alliance

Publications: 1999). Sports courts, fields, and arenas can be so much more than places for keeping kids off the streets. Well-orchestrated school and youth sports programs have the potential of renewing the spirits of participants, teaching life lessons, and strengthening family and community ties.

Selleck, Ph.D., George, *How to Play the Game of Your Life: A Guide to Success in Sports and in Life* (Diamond Communications: 1995). The goal of this book is to help all athletes positively shape their sports experience and use the lessons sports teach to help them succeed in the bigger and more important game of life.

Selleck, Ph.D., George, *Raising a Good Sport in an IN-YOUR-FACE World* (McGraw-Hill: 2002). "George Selleck is one of those rare individuals who is as good a person as he was an athlete, so it is no wonder that he has taken up sportsmanship as a cause."—John Wooden

Shannon, John, *The Coach's Guide to Real Winning: Teaching Life Lessons to Kids in Sports* (Addicus Books: 2001). Ten or fifteen years from now, what will the kids on your team remember? The score of their last tournament game? The number of wins chalked up in their final season? Probably not.

Sheehy, Harry, *Raising a Team Player* (Storey Books: 2002). For every parent that has ever flinched at the sound of a coach screaming at their child, leapt to their feet in outrage at the sight of one player provoking another, silently despaired as an otherwise promising young athlete stormed in tears from a playing field, or watched sadly as an athlete walked away from sports.

Shulman, James L. and William G. Bowen, *The Game of Life: College Sports and Educational Values* (Princeton University Press: 2001). The president of Williams College faces a firestorm for not allowing the women's lacrosse team to postpone exams to attend the playoffs. The University of Michigan loses $2.8 million on athletics despite averaging 110,000 fans at each home football game. Schools across the country struggle with the trade-offs involved with intercollegiate sports.

Silby, Ph.D., Caroline, and Shelly Smith, *Games Girls Play: Understanding and Guiding Youth Female Athletes* (St. Martin's Press: 2000). Many people know that girls who play sports tend to have higher levels of self-esteem than their non-active peers, not to mention fitter, healthier bodies. But few really understand that it takes more than just signing girls up for the neighborhood soccer team to ensure that they get the most out of sports.

Small, MD, Eric, *Kids & Sports: Everything You and Your Child Need to Know About Sports, Physical Activity, and Good Health—A Doctor's Guide for Parents and Coaches* (Newmarket Press: 2002). The only book written for parents by a pediatric sports medicine specialist, this practical, easy-to-read resource on kids and sports offers advice and answers for parents, coaches, teachers, and anyone who deals with children and fitness.

Smith, Dean, *A Coach's Life: My Forty Years in Basketball* (Random House: 1999). For almost forty years, Dean Smith coached the University of North Carolina basketball team with unsurpassed success, having an impact both on the court and in the lives of countless young men.

Smith, Lissa, *Nike Is a Goddess: The History of Women in Sports* (Atlantic Monthly Press: 1998). With the launching of women's professional leagues, the success of Olympic gold medal women's teams, and a new focus on female athletes in the media, women's sports have finally received the attention they have long fought for and rightfully deserve.

Smoll, Frank L., *Way to Go, Coach: A Scientifically Proven Approach to Coaching Effectiveness* (Warde Publishers: 1996). Youth sports are deeply rooted in our social and cultural heritage. Today nearly 25 million youngsters and 3 million adult volunteers participate. *Way to Go, Coach!* celebrates the role of the volunteer coach, recognizing that coaches have unique opportunities for positive impact on young people.

Summitt, Pat, and Sally Jenkins, *Raise the Roof: The Inspiring Story of the Tennessee Lady Vols' Undefeated 1997-1998 Season* (Broadway Books:

1998). "It wasn't a team. It was a tent revival." So says Pat Summitt, the legendary coach whose Tennessee Lady Vols entered the 1997-1998 season aiming for an almost unprecedented "three-peat" of NCAA championships.

Summit, Pat and Sally Jenkins, *Reach for the Summit: the Definite Dozen System for Succeeding at Whatever You Do* (Broadway Books: 1998). Pat Summit, head coach of the University of Tennessee Lady Vols, is a phenomenon in women's basketball. Her ferociously competitive teams won the NCAA championship in 1996 and 1997, and they've won five times in the last ten years.

Thompson, Jim, *Positive Coaching: Building Character and Self-Esteem Through Sports* (Warde Publishers: 1995). *Postive Coaching* is jam packed with specific strategies to address the psychological health of athletes, especially young athletes, in any sport.

Thompson, Jim, *Shooting in the Dark: Tales of Coaching and Leadership* (Warde Publishers: 1998). *Shooting in the Dark* is a philosophical and motivational account of Jim Thompson's two-year tenure coaching a high-school girls basketball team in North Carolina.

VanDerveer, Tara and Joan Ryan, *Shooting from the Outside* (Avon Books: 1997). How a coach and her Olympic team transformed women's basketball. A three-time National Coach of the Year, Tara VanDerveer guided the 1996 U.S. Women's basketball team through an undefeated season of athletic competition culminating in a gold medal win at the Olympic Games in Atlanta.

Walters, John, *The Same River Runs Twice: A Season with Geno Auriemma and the Connecticut Huskies* (Gunkerhalter Press: 2002). "We have the potential this season to be the best women's college basketball squad ever assembled. Anything less than a championship would be a disappointment."—Geno Auriemma

Wilson, Susan, *Sports Her Way: Motivating Girls to Start and Stay with Sports* (Simon and Schuster: 2000). Susan Wilson, a longtime coach and former college gymnastics champion, has written the practical guide for parents who want to encourage their daughters to start—and stay with—sports as a pathway to a lifetime of health and self-esteem.

Wolff, Rick, *Coaching Kids for Dummies* (IDG Books Worldwide: 2000). How do you get kids started in sports? Or provide encouragement without pushing too hard? Or instill a sense of sportsmanship? In this friendly guide, noted sports-parenting authority and Chairman of the Center for Sports Parenting, Rick Wolff provides the answers.

Wolff, Rick, *Good Sports: The Concerned Parents Guide to Competitive Sports* (Dell: 1992). Rick Wolff has written this book to help parents and coaches avoid the pitfalls surrounding the increasingly competitive environment of youth sports while helping children enjoy a positive, challenging and educational sports experience.

Wooden, John, *Wooden: A Lifetime of Observations and Reflections On & Off the Court* (McGraw-Hill: 1997). "I am just a common man who is true to his beliefs."—John Wooden. Evoking days gone by when coaches were respected as much for their off-court performance as for their success on the court, this unique and intimate work presents the timeless wisdom of legendary basketball coach John Wooden.

Wooden, John, *They Call Me Coach* (Contemporary Books: 1998). "What Knute Rockne was to football, Connie Mack to baseball, and Wilbur and Orville Wright to flying, John Wooden is to basketball. This book captures the full flavor of the man, the philosophies that work in life, and the philosophies that work on the court."

Yeager, John, *Character and Coaching—Building Virtue in Athletic Programs* (Dude Publishing: 2001). This book offers practical advice, backed both by the author's personal experience as educator and coach, and by empirical data, on how to create, implement and maintain a character-based athletic program

Yesalis, Charles, *The Steroids Game* (Human Kinetics Publishing: 1998). *The Steroids Game* cuts through the hype and the misinformation common in most books on anabolic steroids. One of the world's top steroid authorities, Charles Yesalis, teams up with Virginia Cowart to provide a straightforward and balanced discussion of what steroids are, how they work, and their affects on athletic performance.

APPENDIX B:
Selected Web Sites on
Sports Parenting

There are more and more Web sites being set up on sports parenting. Here are some of the most helpful.

Center for Sports Parenting (**http://www.sportsparenting.org**)

The Web site that I most strongly suggest is the one that I'm affiliated with. The Center for Sports Parenting, which is based on the campus of the University of Rhode Island and is affiliated with the Institute for International Sport. I strongly urge you go there first with any sports parenting questions you may have.

Athletes for a Better World (**http://www.AforBW.org**)

Athletes for a Better World was founded to address the need for positive mentoring for young people in sport today. Their "Code of Living" requires respect, commitment, dignity, positive influences, sportsmanship, and fair play of all individuals involved in sport.

Character Counts! (**http://www.charactercounts.org**)

Character Counts is a non-profit, nonpartisan, nonsectarian coalition of schools, communities, and non-profit organizations working to advance character education by teaching Six Pillars of Character: trustworthiness, respect, responsibility, fairness, caring and citizenship.

Citizenship Through Sports Alliance (**http://www.sportsmanship.org**)
Officially debuted in 1997, ten school, college, Olympic, and professional
sports league organizations comprise the Citizenship Through Sports
Alliance (CTSA). This organization was formed from a collective concern
about the decline in sportsmanship, ethical conduct in athletics, and a
general malaise pervasive in the current sports culture.

Competitivedge.com **(http://www.competitvedge.com)**
Competitivedge.com is a sports psychology and mental toughness-train-
ing site that offers free resources for athletes, coaches, and parents across
all sports from youth sport to professional. The site offers mental toughness tests, athlete and parent questionaires, peak performance guides, and
a free, monthly, mental toughness newsletter with articles for coaches.

Darell J. Burnett, Ph.D. **(http://www.djburnett.com)**
Dr. Burnett is a clinical sports psychologist, with over 20 years experience
working with children, adolescents, and families in Southern California.
He is the father of three and active as a youth volunteer coach. This Web
site contains his books, articles and audiotapes.

The Institute for the Study of Youth Sports
(http://ed-web3.educ.msu.edu/ysi)
The Institute for the Study of Youth Sports at Michigan State University
was founded by the Michigan Legislature in 1978 to research the benefits
and detriments of participation in youth sports; to produce educational
materials for parents, coaches, officials and administrators; and to provide educational programs for coaches and officials.

Mom's Team **(http://momsteam.com)**
A Web-based resource which provides important and timely information

on youth sports safety, consumer alerts, youth sports equipment and apparel buying tips, and many other youth sports resources to help navigate the sometimes troubled waters of the youth sports experience.

National Alliance for Youth Sports **(http://www.nays.org)**
"Better sports for better kids—better kids for better life"
The National Alliance for Youth Sports, a non-profit organization based in Florida, was founded in 1981 as the National Youth Sport Coaches Association (NYSCA) with the mission of improving out-of-school sports for the more than 20 million youth participants.

National Youth Sports Safety Foundation **(http://www.nyssf.org)**
The National Youths Sports Safety Foundation, Inc. (NYSSF) is a national non-profit, educational organization dedicated to reducing the number and severity of injuries youth sustain in sports and fitness activities. The Foundation is the only organization in the country solely dedicated to this objective.

Positive Coaching Alliance **(http://www.positivecoach.org)**
"Transforming youth sports so sports can transform youth."
The Positive Coaching Alliance (PCA) is an organization based at Stanford University that is trying to change the culture of youth sports, charged with trying to create a positive culture where kids love to play the game and look forward to practice and games.

Sports Doc for Kids **(http://www.sportsdoc4kids.com)**
Founded by Dr. Eric Small, a nationally recognized expert in pediatric and adolescent sports medicine and expert panelist for the Center for Sports Parenting, SportsDoc4kids is a comprehensive Sports Medicine Center Web site for young athletes, dedicated to the prevention and treatment of sports injuries in children and adolescents.

Women's Sports Foundation

(http://www.womenssportsfoundation.org)

Founded in 1974 by Billie Jean King, the Women's Sports Foundation is a charitable, educational organization dedicated to ensuring equal access to and participation and leadership opportunities for all girls and women in sports and fitness. This Web site provides a comprehensive resource for information in education, advocacy, research, and leadership programs.